I0025566

MATT GEORGE

THE
NONPROFIT PROPHET
WHEN COMMUNITY COMES TOGETHER

MVHL

Copyright © 2023 MATT GEORGE

NONPROFIT PROPHET
When Community Comes Together

All rights reserved. No part of this publication may be reproduced, distributed, or transmitted in any form or by any means, including photocopying, recording, or other electronic or mechanical methods, without the prior written permission of the publisher, except in the case of brief quotations embodied in critical reviews and certain other noncommercial uses permitted by copyright law.

For permission requests, write to the publisher, addressed "Attention: Permissions Coordinator" carol@markvictorhansenlibrary.com

Quantity sales special discounts are available on quantity purchases by corporations, associations, and others. For details, contact the publisher at carol@markvictorhansenlibrary.com

Orders by U.S. trade bookstores and wholesalers. Email: carol@markvictorhansenlibrary.com

Creative Contributor - Jennifer Plaza
Cover Design - Low & Joe Creative, Brea, CA 92821
Book Layout - DBree, StoneBear Design

Manufactured and printed in the United States of America distributed globally by markvictorhansenlibrary.com

MVHL

New York | Los Angeles | London | Sydney

ISBN: 979-8-88581-107-1 Hardback
ISBN: 979-8-88581-108-8 Paperback
ISBN: 979-8-88581-109-5 eBook
Library of Congress Control Number: 2023913709

Testimonials

"Matt is the kind of leader you want to follow. He leads with his heart, never loses sight of the greatest outcome possible, and is more gracious than a busload of nuns. His care is the kind of benevolence that's rare and palpable. I am glad to call him a friend and colleague."

— **David Brier, bestselling author of *Brand Intervention* and world-renowned branding expert.**

"Matt George told me about his book, said we must change the narrative, take care of each other, and strive to make every community we live in better. I am a fan and will follow his lead. Be on the lookout for Matt George, the Nonprofit Prophet, coming to a community near you soon. Positive change is what every community needs right now."

— **Shane Needham, Serial Entrepreneur**

"Matt George's expertise shines brilliantly in The Nonprofit Prophet, as he deftly navigates the readers through the intricacies with ease using his profound insights and visionary thinking. This book is an indispensable guide for anyone striving to create a long-lasting impact in the world of nonprofits."

— **David Schoeles, Managing Partner-Chrome Fund, Founder-AB Philanthropy**

"Matt George is a master in the NGO (non-government organization) world by leading in a very business-oriented and collaborative way. He maximizes social impact in the community. Successful communities are the result of the best ROI in all sectors. Matt's leadership and lessons have greatly impacted the most underserved."

— **Michele Sullivan, former President of the Caterpillar Foundation, and author of *Looking Up***

"In Matt's first book Nonprofit Game Plan, I said he was the Nonprofit CEO of our time. In his quest to make change for the better, he now takes on a more important title. He is now The Nonprofit Prophet."

— **Kevin Harrington, an original "Shark" on the hit TV show Shark Tank and Founder of Harrington Enterprises**

"Every community needs a Matt George. He is always fighting for those in need and those who can't. He never stops and never will."

— **Brandon Barnum, CEO of HOA.com and author of *Raving Referrals***

"While change is one of life's foremost challenges, it can be one of our most memorable rewards. In my 30-year Air Force career, our family moved seventeen times—each an enriching chapter. Appreciating Matt's lifelong commitment to his community and his enduring compassion in lifting up the lives of others, I eagerly endorse the Nonprofit Prophet and reflect on our travels through life.

Our Family has come to believe it's not what your Community provides to you; its what you bring to your Community—your values, your passion, you're willing embrace of your neighbors. Enjoy and cherish your own exciting chapters through life!"

— Brigadier General Chip Diehl, US Air Force (Retired)

Dedication

This book is dedicated to Carl George.
He is my mentor, my friend, my rock.
Most important, he is my Father who I love dearly.

Contents

Prologue

Certain books that I read seem to hit home more than others. You all know what I am talking about. An author can grab you and weave a story that places you into the story so to speak. You start visualizing the characters and what they are wearing, what they look like, and even their mannerisms. In *The Nonprofit Prophet*, the characters in a way are real. Even though the characters fit into the fiction category, the story is relatable and happens all over the world daily.

I visualized the characters and the empathy each could represent and then incorporated real life experiences into the book. My goal is to give readers an opportunity to dream and hope for a better society. There are so many people in this world in need. We all know poverty is not going away, but we can at least keep trying to break down pockets and strive to make our world a better place. When I look at the past thirty years and all of the things I have seen in the nonprofit world, it saddens me that at times progress is not being made. Do not get me wrong; there are always success stories and the ones that make you feel good, but as a society—as a world—we need to have more wins.

Running a Children's Home for years helped me realize exactly why people get into our business. It is the impact that each social service employee has on individuals, their communities, and society as a whole. They are the unsung heroes who work overnights, on the streets, responding

to crisis calls at two in the morning, all while facing the violence and the struggles. What keeps everyone coming back is that commitment to make a difference—it is the reason we do what we do. My motto is *Change Lives and Save Lives Daily,* and I truly believe if we all carry that feeling with us every day, then this world will be better.

My hope is that you realize that there are so many rewarding professions, and we need to encourage the younger generation to explore the possibilities of these great careers. We need more people getting into social service work, teaching, healthcare (especially nursing), and special education. We need more speech pathologists, therapists, child psychologists, policemen, and firefighters. There are many more, but you get the picture. Communities, here in America and worldwide, are facing critical shortages and if we work together, we *will* make the change that is so desperately needed.

As you read *The Nonprofit Prophet,* start thinking about just one more thing you can do each day to better someone's life. Change for the better is right around the corner if we work together. Let's change our habits now. Let's work on something to better the lives of the people around us. Stop judging and hating. This is GO time!

Please join me in my vision and realize you too can *Change Lives and Save Lives.*

Matt George
The Nonprofit Prophet

CHAPTER 1

Last Call

"Hey, Cupcake. How's Charlie?" Thomas asked. He already knew the answer—a sentiment to let his only child, and two grandchildren know he was still theirs. All Christine had to do was say the words, and he'd be on the next flight home. He prided himself on his accomplishments in life. And when it came time to get involved in setting up literacy programs around the country. He raised funds for nonprofits that exceeded the attempts his colleagues sought, and in record time. He was a man of honor, and that meant being there for his family. Facing the inevitable, he found a predecessor to the outreach program he started in a small community on the outskirts of Tulsa, Oklahoma. It was his latest ambition, one he was proud of, and confident to hand off. It was only a matter of time.

Thomas's daughter, Christine, whispered through the phone, "I'm losing him, Dad. There's nothing they can do." Her grief came out in sobs that brought tears to Thomas's eyes. He hurt for his little girl, though a grown woman of thirty-four, and his two grandchildren: Jeff and Erika. Charlie was his son-in-law and a man who earned Thomas's deepest respect. He'd gone through hell to fight,

but his brain tumor had other plans. Plans to take him before his fortieth birthday.

Cancer was something Thomas and his family fought against through fundraising for decades. In his youth, Thomas ran marathons after amassing signatures for dollars. Later, his daughter aided him in setting record donations. They would run together for causes all around the country, the world. They even ran in Boston when she was in her second trimester of pregnancy with Jeff. The whole family was involved in charity for all. Charlie worked as a volunteer during an event in Tulsa for the Cancer Society, which is how he and Christine met. Charlie had beaten lymphoma at twelve years of age and worked every event he could manage to get to, once his immune system was strong enough.

Christine ran five events, where she kept seeing his familiar face. And then, after she crossed the finish line at a Chicago marathon, he asked her out for a cupcake. Thomas thought it was cute until she brought home one to share. It was the biggest cupcake either of them had ever seen, and topped with maple bacon. From then on, Thomas's nickname for his daughter was Cupcake. She'd been with Charlie for a decade, and the name flowed off Thomas's tongue.

Holding the phone to his chest, Thomas put it on speaker, wondering if he should stop or continue with the endearment. He was on his way out the door when she called. He was the guest speaker at the annual Adult

Literacy Conference in Tulsa and had to get on the road. His heart ached for Christine as he struggled with being late for the affair. It was a black-tie event with tickets costing upwards of five hundred dollars each. All the proceeds would go into community reading programs for the adults and pressing for better GED training. Too many adults were high school dropouts and too many high schoolers couldn't read at a fifth-grade level.

"Chris, you know I'm here for you and the kids. I'll always be here," Thomas said.

"I know, Dad. And you have to go, or you'll be late. I just wanted to hear your voice."

Thomas pressed his palm to his eye. "Call me if anything changes. I don't care if I'm in the middle of a speech. No decent human being would fault me for being there for my baby girl in her time of need. Hug Jeff and Erika extra tight for me and tell them I said to give you one back, even tighter."

"I will. I love you," she whispered, softer than before.

"Not as much as I love you."

Christine ended the call, leaving Thomas staring at a black screen. His heart, always geared to help, was now being pulled in two directions. He was a self-made man, having founded a hard drive manufacturing plant that he sold for sixty million with residuals. It was enough wealth to last several generations, but it wasn't enough. He had people under his employ that he saw a need to help. He was young and had his whole life ahead of him, which is

how he was able to throw himself into the philanthropic ventures he was so passionate about. Tonight, he needed to get the local people to understand the importance of the human factor when it came to helping their neighbors. A neighbor could be far or near. The semantics didn't matter.

With a city population of just under a half million people, over a million in the metropolitan area, Tulsa was a city tucked into the corner of the state of Oklahoma. The unemployment rate and community service programs went hand in hand. Poverty and illiteracy were factors that affected homelessness, along with senior quality care and crime. Thomas relocated to Tulsa because he wanted to make a difference. As a teenage boy of fifteen, he determined the path he wanted his life to take, but unlike others his age, he followed through. His dreams became reality. If they didn't, then he stayed until a plan was in place to bring his desires to fruition. His advice always was and would be, "No matter what you think, it is my opinion that all people need to have a hand in taking care of each other and their communities that they live in." Thomas was a man with visions and attainable dreams.

What were Thomas's dreams? It didn't involve driving a race car, unless it was for charity, or even to become rich and famous. His goal was to find the pockets of need hidden in the deepest trenches of American cities. It started with a single marathon for the Cancer Association and grew to encompass over two hundred seventy-five events by his sixtieth birthday. As long as one adult could not

read, Thomas would not rest. Children with cancer and no means to pay for treatment, homeless veterans, and hungry families haunted his dreams. He saw them when others passed them by.

He even created a formula for devising a budget to keep over two hundred employees at a facility in Los Angeles for children—before he got to Oklahoma. And it wasn't on a whim how he got there. Thomas heard about a fundraiser for a town destroyed by an EF5 tornado not far from the city. He planned to give the community a check to match the donations of surrounding towns and communities. When he asked his assistant to arrange the flight, she asked him if this would be the first time he offered his services in that state. He paused to remember all the events and realized he'd only passed through. It prompted him to do a quick inquiry into what cities had a history that seeded poverty. Tulsa landed on his radar.

After raising the funds for the tornado survivors, he settled in a small town outside of Tulsa and began the work that promised to change the lives of many people. Just as it had been in New York, Massachusetts, Florida, Texas, California, Arizona, New Mexico, Alabama, Georgia, and nearly each state in the U.S., he created a vision. One that would reach across the classes and show support to those who felt sorrow and shame.

All too often, Thomas came across a sibling pair who lost their parents and were living on the streets. Or he found homeless teenagers who ran away from abusive homes

and would rather endure the crime, hunger, and elements than to face the belt, or worse. He learned parents could be cruel, untrusting people. But he also learned that parents could be the most loving, devoted beings who lost their child to addiction. Sometimes, those parents would fall victim to the addiction from guilt and grief. It was a matter of mental health, homelessness, addiction, suicide prevention, and a wealth of other factors that crossed boundaries. Meeting a single need was not enough.

He developed a plan that allowed his nonprofit organizations to build a budget that supported the programs and the employees. He held job interviews with the prospects for open positions, focusing on the career aspect rather than the get rich side of working. There were rewards to be reaped that ran deeper than money. Volunteering at the farm stand in downtown, in any city, where the food is cheaper, he witnessed mothers with six or more children to feed, buy a single vegetable to last for the week. Extended families were a big part of culture in many of those areas. When the food pantry had access to fresh produce, he made sure to have those mothers and fathers and elder siblings take as much as they dared.

Thomas also learned that he could not push people because they chose to be humble. One time, while passing through a somewhat ghost town in South Carolina, he saw a row of small houses in need of repair. They should have been cottages, but they were too small and too dilapidated. Two women sat on plastic buckets selling boiled peanuts.

They had no shoes, and their dresses were worn thin. He bought all the peanuts and gave them back to the women to feed their families. He also hired several local young men to put a roof on the homes that needed them. He started a housing project in that town by getting the local business owners involved in community betterment. He even negotiated a job for one of the women at the hardware store he bought the supplies from. The owner took the names of the men hired by Thomas and used them when customers asked for home improvement contractors. It was a small-scale example of Thomas's effect on humanity, community, and commitment.

But now he had a new mission.

Thomas stuffed his cellphone in his jacket pocket and headed out to the livery car. He ducked inside with his tux coat folded over his arm, careful not to drop the phone. It would be a close call, but he'd make it to the conference in time to walk on stage. After Christine's call, he knew tonight would be the last event he attended in Tulsa, and the one where he had to say 'goodbye.'

"Good evening, Mr. Thomas," the valet said, opening the car door for Thomas. He slipped the tux jacket on before stepping out. It started to rain, so the young man held the umbrella out for Thomas to keep his attire dry and his blue patent leather oxfords shined.

"Thank you, Jim," Thomas said. "You're going to need it for yourself."

"Don't worry about me, sir. Have a good evening." Jim

walked with Thomas to the doors and kept the umbrella over his charge until he was inside the backstage door off the alley. The important guests and speakers entered the back to avoid encounters with fans of a sort. There were always people who wanted to ask for advice, or to get a picture with him. Although he was happy to do so, Thomas knew he had a speech to deliver. After, he would spend a good hour meeting and greeting eager patrons. It warmed him through when he interacted with them because those were the ones who went on to spread the philanthropic ideology. They absorbed the details of Thomas's plans and sometimes even started programs to match his own.

Thomas ducked through the green steel door into a gray metal stairwell. He'd spoken at the center before and knew he had to go up a flight to get to the green room behind the stage. There was no time to find his seat, it would have to wait. He checked his hair in the mirror, smoothed the several wild white strands into place and straightened his bowtie. He had his speech notes on his phone, ready. As he glanced over them, he heard the muffled announcement. The stage manager hurried him to stage left and clipped a mic to his jacket.

"Ladies and gentlemen, it is my pleasure to introduce the man behind the mission. The nonprofit prophet himself, Mr. Thomas Matthews."

Thomas smiled, waved at the room filled with tables and the standing applause. The amount of support would never cease to amaze him, nor would it fail to fill his heart

with warmth, knowing the people in the room understood. And that was how he planned his speech, acknowledging the human factor.

"Thank you, all," he said. The crowd hushed. "But do not applaud me. Look around the room. Each and every one of you is here for a cause. A reason that goes beyond selflessness. Let us applaud one another, friend, and neighbor. Colleague and partners." Applause overtook his voice. He smiled at the crowd and motioned with his hands for the room to settle down. The people took their seats and Thomas began. "As you know, illiteracy is an issue that shouldn't be. Adults who cannot read a newspaper cannot fill out a job application. They cannot read the gas pump, or their child's homework and letters from the school. Imagine, if you will, a man in his twenties having his daughter bring her spelling list home to practice and showing it to him." Several members in the audience shook their heads. They knew who he was talking about. It was an actual story, but Thomas would never disclose the person's identity. "You know what it feels like to not know something that someone thinks you should. We all do. It's uncomfortable. We, as humans, do not want to admit that we do not know. We would rather say something, anything, than to face the truth, and utter those three little words, 'I don't know.' Think about that."

He paused for several breaths.

"Now imagine that your six-year-old comes to you, their parent. They're excited to read. They're gonna learn,

and they're going to get a gold star on the chart because the teacher knew they studied. They went over their words with Daddy." He scanned the room. "But Daddy can't spell. He can't read the list. He feels shame, like a failure. It makes him angry, and maybe sends her to her room to do her homework. He doesn't have time for that. The little girl goes to school the next day, and the teacher asks, 'Did you study your list?' and the little girl lies. She is afraid to tell the truth because all the other kids said they did. She says, 'Yes.' The teacher goes on with the lessons. A year passes by, and the girl is falling farther behind. She can't read the phonics books. She doesn't do the assignments where she must find pictures in a magazine at home and paste them on a page, because her father doesn't buy magazines. He can't read them, and he doesn't have the money left over from his paycheck for him to spend."

Thomas stepped back from the podium and walked to the front of the stage. "Adult illiteracy is child illiteracy. The effects snowball. Eventually, one or both give up. In this case, the teacher called a conference with the father, and he disclosed his own issue. She took it upon herself to help that young father so that he could read. That woman also stayed after school to work with the student, who went on to be accepted into the National Honor Society. But it gets better. As a part of her community service, she started a literacy outreach at her local library, where several of the NHS members go to help teach reading and writing to the community. This is why we are here tonight. To put these

programs into place and to guide the young people into a future where they can identify a need and not be afraid of being part of the solution." Thomas made his way back behind the podium. The phone in his pocket vibrated, once, twice. He reached in and pulled it out. "My question to all of you is this: what more can we do? What other solutions might there be? Thank you." He bowed his head toward the room and rushed off stage, accepting the call.

"Chris?"

"Dad, he's gone."

CHAPTER 2

Endurance

T homas's condo in Near West Side was a welcome change from his ranch outside Tulsa, though he hadn't welcomed the reason. Losing his son-in-law, Charlie, meant it was time to redirect his focus. In all his philanthropic years, family was a nonnegotiable factor. They came first, no matter how it tugged at his gut. He was an intelligent man who understood poverty and the problems that came with it. It was not going to be solved overnight. He had to trust the people he handpicked to take over each platform, of which there were many.

This new position required a different level of intimacy with the subject, his relationship with spousal loss. His daughter's call brought back the same fear that flushed through him when he'd learned of his wife's passing. He did not wish it on her or his grandchildren, but as Thomas understood, life was not there to be fair. It was an experience. And in his experience, he knew that loss left a lot of people homeless, lost, or addicted. He saw orphans on the street, sets of siblings trying to navigate their way, and mothers with starving infants in their arms.

One time at a conference in Michigan, he heard a woman ask another attendee, "How can a child be homeless? Aren't there laws?" It made Thomas realize how ignorant society was to the world outside of their little boxes. The ones

lucky enough to ask were people who did not understand what was right underneath their own noses. Or they did not want to know with what horrors really existed. It was not propaganda, a political motion, or ploy.

The question unnerved him, but it caused him to change his speech. That night, when he took the stage, he started talking about child abuse: the neglect, the poverty, the need for assistance when children were put into the foster system. Then, he said, "Did you know—there are homeless children?" He paused for the audience to absorb his question. "The McKinney-Vento Homeless Assistance Act clarified what it means for a child to be considered homeless—not having a place to call their own, for the night. That means being thrown out of their parent's house, running away, couch surfing, sleeping anywhere or living in a place that is not their home. Now some may think that these are the kids who are delinquents, but many are from abused homes. They flee their abusers."

Thomas remembered the murmurs that rumbled through the audience that day as he gazed at the trees outside of his building. He knew there were children on Chicago's streets, as well as adults who were thrust into situations they weren't ready for. He stepped out onto the balcony. He loved traveling, but not moving. Getting settled took time unless he threw himself into work.

He stepped back inside, closed the doors, and thought about his next adventure. His daytime schedule was free, and there were people in need. He pulled a map of Chicago

from his carry-on bag and spread it over the granite topped island in the kitchen. He circled the area in the southwestern section of his neighborhood near where his daughter and grandchildren lived. It was a middle-class area with a school that served a mixed class student body. If he was going to make a difference, it was a good bet that he'd get his start by scanning the district borders.

Chicago had seventy-seven communities and over 600 schools. Experience taught him that narrowing down meant focusing on a controllable outcome. To Thomas, the outcome was the goal, both short- and long-term. His direction had to be aimed at helping the community. Perhaps he would target literacy, or maybe homelessness. He wasn't sure what he would encounter, but the last several cities had a déjà vu vein of neglect. One that he wanted to tap and heal.

Thomas wandered to the lobby of his five-story condo after checking in with his daughter. He promised to do so, because it was her first day back at work after the funeral. The salon was a small room with a Chippendale sofa and a digital bulletin board. He took a seat, taking the time to learn about the events in the area, and of any programs he may find interesting. To his surprise, one piqued his interest. A neighborhood enrichment meeting was scheduled in the conference room. He took a picture of the bulletin board with his cell phone. "On the lower level, seven o'clock," he muttered.

A middle-aged woman dressed in a soft pink silk blouse and white skirt stopped at his side. Her small white

fascinator hid the side of her face. She had to turn to look at Thomas as she spoke. "Excuse me, Mr.?"

Thomas stood, extending his hand. "Thomas Matthews."

She held his fingers, an incomplete shake of sorts. "Elize Noqua, a pleasure." She pulled her hand back to hold her clutch. "I was just on my way to pick up my son from school. But I saw you take a photo. Do you plan on attending the meeting this evening?"

"I do," Thomas acknowledged.

Elize smiled. "Wonderful. I am the committee chair and always welcome our new residents. It promises to be a good one. We're discussing the new homeless shelter."

That caught Thomas's attention. It was perfect. He would wait to offer his expertise until he assessed the room. But he felt good about his new venture. It was off to a running start. "Then I am most excited to attend. I assume the lower level means the basement?"

She smiled. "It sounds abysmal when it's called that. I prefer the lower level. It brightens things up." She glanced at her watch, a silver sliver of jewelry on her wrist. "See you tonight!" She hurried out of the building.

He knew his grandchildren, Jeff and Erika, would be getting home soon. He decided to walk to their house, to get a feel for the neighborhoods. He went back to his apartment to get his tawny long coat and hat. Chicago wasn't called the Windy City for nothing. Being early autumn, the trees were still green, and the grass was green, but the cold

off the lake made it feel later in the season. There were a few clouds graying the sky, but nothing threatening. Though he took his umbrella for good measure. He wouldn't have thought it odd if he saw the first snow flurries of the season.

Walking was a habit Thomas formed when he first started city improvement planning. It gave him an idea of boundaries, borders, lifestyles, and culture. The smell of garlic permeated the air from a nearby family-style Italian restaurant. It tantalized his senses. Near West Side was beautiful, with neat rows of houses, iron work, clean sidewalks, and small condos. The cars ranged from Bentleys to BMWs. His older Cadillac was fine, but he was considering a possible replacement. Not that he was leaning toward one brand or the other, but he was thinking something with brawn for the weather.

He headed down the sidewalk, wondering how the kids were doing without the façade they put on for their mother. Thomas understood children well because he remembered when his own father passed when he was in high school. Although they were still in middle school, he was aware of the strength they wished to demonstrate while supporting their mother.

Since Christine was a social worker for the state, she got off work at four-thirty in the afternoon. Her office was in the heart of downtown Chicago. In many of their calls, she spoke of Little Village having a large minority population in an impoverished area. She also spoke of the West Side, and how her heart ached for the people.

Thomas decided to wait until the meeting before diving into his research. The prospect of offering his expertise on the subject overjoyed him, as he felt his closure in Tulsa was abrupt. One issue he wanted to learn more about was one close to Christine's heart. Something he'd learned not more than a month back, during one of their late-night chats which became more frequent as Charlie's health declined.

"Dad, it hurts. This job is not for the faint of heart, I'll tell you that," she had said.

"Want to fill me in?" he asked.

Christine sighed into the phone. "I guess. Charlie is asleep on the sofa and I tucked the kids in. I've got the room to myself and not feeling the wind down. My mind is running on high."

Thomas poured himself a glass of merlot, settled into his armchair with a leather-bound journal and pen, poised to make a record of the information. "I'm listening."

"Well," she started, "I keep getting these cases. The kids are so thin. Too sick for school, a boy went truant. The mother was nowhere to be found. The truancy officer found him. He died of malnutrition."

"I'm sorry, Chris. Sometimes I have no answers, but that doesn't mean a solution for the future is impossible. Hunger is a problem in every country on God's green earth. If there is enough money to fund a stadium or to buy HD televisions for political offices, there is enough for families to have the assistance they need."

Thomas regrouped, feeling his blood pressure rise.

"Hunger is needless, with all the food waste from manufacturing facilities, restaurants, and stores. The wasted food alone would solve world hunger. Okay, rant over. Listen, I don't need superpowers to know that Chicago is hurtin'. North Lawndale is one."

"He was seven," she whispered into the phone. "We took the siblings into custody, but that's all I can say about it."

"You say what you can. But be proud of the difference you make. Social work is service work. You'll never get rich from it," Thomas reminded.

Chris laughed half-heartedly, burdened by a breaking heart and unable to comprehend others' treatment of their children. "I'm not it for the money. None of us are. Once you see the conditions these kids endure, you fight for them. You stand up for them because they're too scared or weak to do it themselves. My job doesn't end at 4:30 just because the state says so. The reality is hours were always hard because they were sometimes dictated by crisis and working when needed. My point is this job is not easy and I always felt like I was on call 24/7 no matter what the hours stated."

"I've said it before, and I'm saying it again. I'm proud of you, Cupcake."

They hung up the phone and Thomas finished his wine while researching community gardens on his phone. There were dilapidated buildings next to vacant lots, making the

perfect location to create a free food source. He believed in communities helping themselves and their neighbors.

With his walk winding down as he approached Christine's house, he realized he'd daydreamed about their talks more than he noticed the streets. It didn't matter because he knew what needed to be done. He already had an idea for a plan to present at the meeting.

Thomas knew the questions to ask. He vowed to himself, "Tonight, the people in New Lawndale will be heard."

CHAPTER 3

Cookies

Christine walked through the door, her motherly smile in place. Thomas was in the kitchen slicing tomatoes for the dinner salad. Erika had put the lasagna that Chris had prepped the night before into the oven as Thomas supervised. It was his favorite dish, which he just happened to tell his daughter in one of their midnight talks. It lightened his heart when he arrived at their brick abode, met the kids, and was taken by Erika to see the glorious masterpiece. She wore her heart in her smile. He planned to take them out, but as Thomas told Chris when she walked in, "Your homemade lasagna is better than any restaurant's grub in all Chicago."

Thomas locked eyes with Chris and he saw her face relax. He knew the creases that manifested from stress. He recognized them in his own daughter's forehead, along with the darkened patches beneath her eyes. Chris was always beautiful and looked like her mother. *And nothing will ever change that,* he thought. But it hurt him to see his daughter age beyond her young years. She still had half a decade before she reached forty.

Chris smiled at her father. "Thanks, Dad. But if you asked these two, they'd probably pick garlic knots or pizza and wings."

Thomas went to her and kissed her head. He was a solid six feet, one hundred and eighty pounds. She was on the shorter side, five feet three inches, and thick dark brown hair that she kept swept in a loose bun. It was easy for him to kiss her head and offer comfort. He wrapped his arms around her. "I would never choose pizza over my girl's cookin'," He glanced at the kids and winked.

The tangy aroma of the lasagna filled the house with a blend of tomatoes, garlic, and melting cheese. One of Thomas's emotional outlets was cooking, a trait he passed on to his daughter. Simmering sauces for eight hours on a weekend led to delicious meals at the ready for the month. He loved that his grandchildren were learning the same skill and carrying on family recipes. While Jeff set the table, Erika grabbed the lasagna from the oven. Christine was just about to help her when the pan slipped from the fabric oven mitts.

The lasagna hit the floor, red sauce splattering everywhere.

Erika gasped with a squeal. Thomas turned in time to see the enamel pan hit. Jeff rounded the corner of the kitchen island, sliding in his socks.

"Score!" he shouted. "Betcha couldn't do that again."

The pan landed right side up. It had been more of a direct fall than a flip. Thomas went to get the pan, but Chris beat him to it.

"No, bother. This is a blessed dinner for sure." She took

a kitchen towel from the counter and grabbed the ends. "Well, that was exciting."

Thomas laughed, "Hmm, you sure it wasn't a ploy for pizza?" He winked at his granddaughter, handing her a paper towel. As the girl wiped the sauce off the floor, Thomas blotted the red droplets on his pants. He had a meeting that evening and needed to go home to change. An hour for dinner would give him time to enjoy the visit and still make it back to his apartment.

The four sat around the oak dining table. Christine dished the lasagna while Thomas passed the salad. The lasagna incident brought back normalcy. He noted the kids laughing and smiling while their mother joked. It was genuine, good-natured banter. They were going to be alright.

Thomas got up to leave after the kids cleared the table. Christine offered to give him a ride, but Thomas liked to get a feel for the streets—to go into the areas most were afraid to go, and to peek in the alleys. He wanted to experience different cultures and living situations, to get a better idea how he could help. He enjoyed being aware. The walk home was chilly, but the sky cleared. He kept his umbrella tucked under his arm, following the sidewalks. People were in their homes. The streets were quiet. After what he read, he thought there would be more activity. He reached his building and went up to his apartment.

#

After changing into a navy sport coat, over a white

polo shirt, and navy slacks, Thomas donned his blue suede shoes. Since they were his trademark, he had packed several pairs. Once he arrived at his destination, he took the elevator to the lower level. The carpeted hall had a set of double doors propped open. He wandered over, checking to see if it was the right room. He recognized Elize. She'd changed into a black skirt suit. Her black hair was up in a clip.

"Hello, need any help?" he offered. He didn't expect she did, but it was the icebreaker he needed to get her to lower her guard. The chairs were already in place, the long table for the board was at the front of the room, and the side table displayed bakery boxes filled with Italian cookies and a plate of brownies.

"No, I think we're all set." She laughed. "Well, we still need people."

Thomas nodded. "Ah, always the tough part." He pointed to the plate of brownies. "These look fantastic. Are they local?"

Elize smiled, "Come get a cup of coffee, and grab one. They're not just for show. I go to Maria's, about three blocks over. Their pastries are to die for."

"Make it green tea, and you've got a deal," Thomas chided. Green tea was his personal addiction, which he often drank three or more cups a day.

The kind woman pointed to a carafe marked "hot water" with a wooden box of assorted teas beside the hotplate. "You're in luck. Help yourself."

Thomas took an out-of-place tricolor packet and made

a cup of green tea. While pouring, he realized someone had wisely integrated warm tones into the décor, creating trust. It was a nonthreatening environment. Soft yellows and creams were already in place from the paint on the walls and the trim. The tablecloth was white linen with gold embroidery edges. Elize had banners hung with the words: live, love, and give. *Undoubtedly*, he thought, *she's a helper. She was trained in the art of mindful exercise.* He wondered if she was a counselor. He learned to build trust in his own years of training and recognized the signs.

"Have you held many meetings of this sort before?" he asked.

Elize took a biscotti and straightened the row. As she pressed the tap on the coffee urn, she elaborated with a bit of history. "Mr. Thomas, this meeting is one of many I've held here for our small building. The one for the community has a larger turnout, but it gets well over a hundred attendees. We'll be lucky to see twenty residents tonight. I choose my battles."

"What do you mean?" He finished the tea and poured himself another. "What are we talking about?"

She sighed, "Let's just say there is a lot of need in Chicago, and sometimes crime sneaks its way into giving hearts. Kind people fear their safe cocoon being infiltrated by outsiders that promise unknown futures. They want undeniable proof that their safe havens will remain safe."

Thomas understood. It was a common and valid concern everywhere he spoke. But never enough to warrant

a heads up from a fellow giver. "I'd like to go to one of those meetings."

"You're in luck. Next Monday, at seven. The brick building by the town hall. Second floor. I'll make the announcement after tonight's meeting."

He sipped his green tea. "So, what's your interest? I study all the links in the chain myself, but you chose a homeless shelter. I'm just curious why?" He sat in one of the cream and gold chairs crossing his ankle over his knee. "You intrigue me, Ms. Elize."

Elize smiled and sipped her own coffee. "Funny you should ask." She checked her phone. "We've got a few minutes. I guess it would help. Everyone coming already knows my passion." She took the seat next to him. "I started out as a salon owner, expanded to a full-service day spa. Opened twelve locations in three counties. It was great. I felt good, you know?"

Thomas nodded.

"Then, one night, the receptionist at my first establishment called me." Elize's eyes blurred with unshed tears. "She had to call the police. Outside of my door, right there on the sidewalk, lay a scruffy gentleman. Many times, he would be searching for scraps in the city garbage cans, or wandering up the alley between the buildings. We never spoke, but I wish we had. He passed away from hypothermia. The winter temperatures were too cold for his threadbare coat, and he fell asleep against the brick façade of my storefront. He was seeking shelter under the

awning." She put the coffee on the chair next to her. "I never asked him in or reached out to see what I could do. After he passed away in front of my salon, a plethora of questions flooded my mind."

"Homelessness is an issue that plagues the world. You need to focus on the fact that you chose to change. That man was the catalyst to your philanthropic fortitude. How much have you raised so far? In your giving career?"

"Not including my own donations, I dedicate all funds from that particular store to the community, two hundred fifty thousand. I always give it to the shelters, but I want to start my own—one that can be a self-sustaining entity—one that will outlast me."

A young man entered the room. He had on a pair of gray slacks, black chukka boots, and a yellow polo shirt. He sat in the second row of chairs and leaned toward them. "Sorry to interrupt."

"Don't be silly, Ron. This is Mr. Thomas Matthews. He's new to Near West."

He stood and offered his hand to Thomas. "I'm Ronald Gremle, her son."

Thomas shook his hand. "A pleasure. It's good to see young people get involved."

Soon after, nine other young people drifted in and headed toward the refreshment table. They took their coffees and cookies back to their chairs and sat. The soft murmur of their chatter grew louder in the room. Thomas took joy in watching the hope of the future, sharing,

laughing, and discussing the fate of New Lawndale, one brick at a time. After the meeting, he left with an invitation to join the community meeting and was offered space at the food pantry. He'd be handing out whole chickens donated each week by one of the other residents. With his motivation running high, he walked home and poured himself a glass of sweet tea before collapsing in his recliner. Instead of waiting for Christine to call, he rang her first.

"Dad?"

"Hey, Chrissy," Thomas sighed.

"Is something wrong?"

"Actually, quite the opposite. I feel good. Sometimes, you just need to share the joy." Thomas sat back and sipped the tea and filled her in on Elize and Ron and the upcoming meeting. "Now that we have a moment to talk, how was your day?"

"Not as good, I'm afraid. We just don't have the staff. Social work is unforgiving, it hurts, and it's raw. We have a high turnover rate. It seems like no one wants to work in the field anymore." She laughed, "I guess you always told me I needed a soft heart and tough skin for a reason."

"How about you join me at a meeting next Monday? It's a few blocks from your house, by the town hall," Thomas asked.

Christine sighed into the phone. "Yeah, why not? It's been a while since I got involved around here."

The father and daughter ended their call, intent on making a change one brick at a time. And just to make a

good impression, Thomas decided to purchase a large order of assorted cookies from Maria's. *And maybe*, he thought, *they'll be willing to donate to the food pantry.* Baby steps for the community businesses was how he planned to share his agenda. An agenda that meant more than a shelter. One that offered a higher quality of life and showing people they had a way out. But he would save that for a future meeting.

#

Monday arrived, and Thomas met Chris outside of the town hall building. Maria's had donated two hundred cookies to match the two hundred Thomas bought. He planned to give the leftovers to the food pantry. He was pulling the boxes from his Cadillac when Chris tapped him on the shoulder.

"What's up?" He stood and looked in the direction his daughter was facing. Her eyes were wide. Thomas's chest tightened. It took a moment to realize the group in front of the building wasn't waiting to get in.

"Dad, they're picketing!" Chris exclaimed.

"I see that." Thomas took the two paper bags with the cookies, one in each hand. "Follow me and don't stop." He made his way to the brick building where the meeting was to take place. He was half an hour early and knew that they were there to stop the shelter. "Not going to lie, Chris. I didn't expect this."

Chris shrugged. "Let's do it," she said.

Thomas raised the paper bags at his sides and charged forward through the small crowd of about thirty. "Good evening, folks. The milk and cookies are on me." He pushed his way through and opened the metal door to the building. He stepped aside for Chris to enter and turned to face the crowd, but before going in, someone threw a rock which hit him on the chin. A few drops of blood dripped onto his hand.

CHAPTER 4

Sticks and Stones

Outside the meeting hall doors, the group of angry protesters pressed in around Thomas. The gash on his chin was small, but it was enough for him to realize the blood on his face was the instigator for the growing agitation in the crowd. He heard one woman yell, "It's a young boy and his sister. They're running."

Thomas looked up in time to see the two youths as they took off. To Thomas, they appeared to be the athletic sort. He didn't want to cause more of a scene at an already touchy juncture. He hadn't even attended his first meeting on the subject, and now he needed to play mediator to keep escalations from getting out of hand.

The crowd moved as a mass of pristine blazers, university themed hoodies, and everything in between. They maneuvered between parked cars and spilled onto the quiet street. It was evening, and the hall was closed, except for the meeting that was yet to take place. To be honest, Thomas hadn't thought there would be a turnout to speak of, let alone a protest. He didn't even know where the structure in question was to be introduced. He was getting to know the neighborhood, but needed to find out the location of the proposed building.

"Let them go," Thomas called over the murmurs. He turned to Chris and whispered loud enough for her to hear

over the excitement. "How can you be angry at a couple of kids when you have a hostile mob rushing the door and hollering at people in the streets?"

Chris agreed, "I know. Peaceful protests have differing meanings to various people. How is a child supposed to understand the causes behind yelling, banging, and a crowd of people being obnoxious?" The crowd hollered and a group of women knocked over a garbage can. They were moving toward the young men who returned with the boy walking ahead of him.

The violence is already happening, Thomas thought. He pulled a white handkerchief from his back pocket and blotted the smarting wound on his chin. When he pulled it away, there was a small red blotch. "Damn it," he sighed.

"Leave him alone," a familiar voice to Thomas screamed. It was Elize. She ran to the child and took his hand, leading him away from the angry mob.

"Elize?" Thomas yelled.

The stout woman looked up. "Thomas?"

Thomas set his bags down and pushed through the people, stopping in the middle of the street where he crouched before the child. "Are you alright?" he asked the lad.

Tears had dried on the child's mocha cheeks. Elize removed a small packet of tissues from her pocket, pulling one free. "What's going on, Thomas?"

"Why don't we ask this young man?" he replied.

Elize blotted the youth's eyes. "Pobrecito, que paso?"

Fresh tears wet the long black lashes. The boy tucked

his chin, his lips peeled back as he sobbed, exposing his toothless visage. "Lo siento," he cried.

Christine caught up to them, the crowd forming a circle in the street. A police siren grew louder as it approached. She put her hand out for the little boy. "My name is Christine. We want to learn what made you so angry, but we need to move out of the road to do that. Would you like to take this nice lady's hand and follow her?"

The boy nodded.

Elize led him between two cars to the sidewalk next to a tree. "This will give him some space from the onlookers."

Thomas left them to focus on the crowd. He knew protests well. He was also familiar with partaking in them. Having been on both sides of the fence, he tapped into the reasoning that was settling back into the growing crowd. He raised his volume so they could hear. "No doubt this evening was uncalled for, but it's over. The police are on it now. Let's get back to the business we all came to discuss. If you would follow me." He motioned with his hand and led the way to the building, not sure which way he was supposed to go once inside. He just wanted the people to redirect their overexcited emotions.

Sure enough, they followed, single filing up the stairs. An elderly woman of African American descent pointed at the ceiling above her. "The room is to the left, second floor, second door."

Thomas shook his head to acknowledge her and led the way.

The meeting room was much larger than he expected. Someone propped open the wooden double doors. The tongue and groove floor transitioned to beige tile. Metal folding chairs sat aligned in rows. A long white table with a wooden podium propped in the middle was at the head. A banner hanging from the center had a circle of hands with the words: friendship, community, compassion.

Thomas found a center seat in the front row. An angry woman with pitch-black hair pulled into a neat bun, secured with a decorative pin and wearing a white pant-suit, sat next to him. "Patricia Loggins," she said, pulling the fingers of her white gloves. Once they were off, she offered Thomas her hand. "I do hope the wound doesn't scar. Nasty child. That's why we're here. We can't have that sort, infiltrating our community."

Thomas cocked his brow. "I believe the child was responding to what he does not understand in the only way he knew. He wanted to be heard."

Patricia frowned. "I don't care about his reason. And where are his parents? A child that age, running the streets? It's ridiculous."

"I wonder," he said, pausing for dramatic flair. "If he has parents."

Patricia settled into her uncomfortable seat, folded her hands, and fiddled with her gold ring, repositioning the stone. Thomas knew it was a way to avoid further discussion, which meant she understood his stand on the issue. He made his point.

After the meeting, which turned out to be a screaming match, Thomas and Christine ducked out of the building ahead of the mass of angry residents. The main takeaway that Thomas got was that bringing in low income and homeless housing had the potential to invite more crime to the area. Several men and women used the evening's incident to make their case. One man had taken a picture of the kids while the daughter of an angry women shot a video of the event as it happened.

The board members implored Thomas to file a report with the police, but he refused. Elize and Chris joined the meeting after it was in full swing. They had remained with the officers and the small boy. Taking the open seats next to Thomas, they filled him in during a break.

"Thomas, the police were called," Elize whispered. "I had to give them all the information I knew. I'm sick for the poor grandmother."

"Just how well do you know this boy?" Thomas asked, keeping his voice to a hushed minimum in order to keep the attention away from their discussion.

Elize frowned, "Too well. I recognized the boy right away. I've seen him more times than I can count. He assists his grandmother to the food pantry and carries the bags for her."

"But isn't that during school hours?" Christine interrupted.

"It is," Elize affirmed. "But that's just it. His grandma is elderly and disabled. Really, Gabe is a very good boy. He's

a wonderful grandson and should not be plagued by the anger when his little plate is already so full."

Thomas sighed, "He's probably overwhelmed by the hostility exhibited by the protesters. Good thing he and his grandmother aren't in here tonight."

Elize frowned, "He's eight-years-old, Thomas. All he understands is that his grandma is being evicted from her apartment because she couldn't pay the rent. She has no extra funds. His mother died of a heroin overdose and his father is an unknown. Gabe takes care of his grandma and his sister, but never talks about it because he's afraid the school will have him taken away. He heard his grandma talking to me about a low-income place and I pushed her to get on the waitlist."

Thomas went silent during an outburst by a man in favor of the shelter. He couldn't help but agree that the situations faced by the impoverished neighborhoods afforded no opportunities for respite. It reminded him of a woman back in Tulsa who used to collect unused food from other mothers, mainly peanut butter and beans, which she used to make cookies. She sold them on the sidewalk outside of the churches. The woman made a few dollars to spend on her children. The priest allowed her to hold her bake sale even without a permit because he did not want to take away the little piece of hope she had left. But a few people alerted the authorities. The police issued a fine and then chased her away. The priest paid the fine, and from then on, bought all her goods to serve his parishioners.

"Dad," Christine said, getting Thomas's attention back to the conversation in the car. "The meeting is over. You must put the issues aside for one night. You always throw yourself into your work. It's important to take time for you. You're no good to anyone without proper rest and that mind of yours never shuts off."

Thomas laughed, "Fine. Tell you what, tomorrow you said the kids are going to their friends' houses to spend the night. I'll pick you up at six and we'll go to the Signature Room."

"Over the top a bit, don't you think?" she laughed.

He shrugged, "Always."

CHAPTER 5

Soup's On

Thomas donned a black suit with a fat tie and diamond tack. He practiced the routine he made from the time she was just a little thing. It started with a father-daughter dance at school and evolved into going out on little dates. At first, they were a venture her mother insisted upon.

"You want her to grow up knowing how to be treated by a man," she'd said.

Thomas felt awkward standing in their kitchen dressed in his finest suit, waiting for his little Christine to emerge. But the moment she stepped over the threshold dressed in a lime green princess gown with her eyes lighting her tiny face, he realized his wife was right. He never wanted their daughter to lose that joyous light.

And as he did all those years ago, Thomas donned his best suit to pick up his little girl. But instead of being a princess, she chose a plain black dress with pearls and a broach that was her mother's.

He drove up in his black Cadillac, parked on the street, and hurried to the other side to open her door as she come out the front door. Chris held her clutch in front of her and smiled at him as she got in and made herself comfortable. He drove them to the Signature Room, one of Chicago's

finest dining establishments located in the John Hancock building.

The restaurant loomed over the city with panoramic views. It was over ninety floors high, and had white linen tables, a gourmet menu, and the place where he first took Chris on their father-daughter date. They hadn't been back since. When Thomas made the reservation, he was excited to see the changes in the establishment and on the menu, but not so much with his daughter, because she had grown.

The young woman joining him was not the little princess who smiled too hard for her cheeks. Living in different cities meant more phone calls than real visits. She had changed into a professional woman with a few gray hairs and creases at the corners of her mouth. He could see her face in his grandchildren. Try as he might, he did not see himself in them, but in conviction he did. He was proud of the family he raised.

He parked in the garage on Chestnut, and they walked together side by side. Both wore light jackets as protection against the cool evening air. Once inside the lobby, they took the elevator to the famous restaurant. The host had their table reserved. For Thomas, it was a way to enjoy time with his daughter and to pluck at her thoughts. He knew that when the kids were safe from their sleepovers and happy with friends, Christine let her guard down. Just like their late-night phone calls, she would unfold a wealth of ideas and concerns.

"Hey, Dad. Whatcha thinking about?" Christine asked.

Thomas tugged the corners of his mouth up. "Nothing. Everything."

"Come on, spill."

He sighed, sipped his green tea, and leaned forward. "Enjoying old memories. You look so much like your mom now. I'm a lucky man to have had your mom, you, and the kids. Money didn't give me that."

Chris flaked her salmon apart and slid the small morsel into her mouth. "True, but it did give the world to you."

Christine's words tugged at something inside Thomas. He didn't feel like he did enough. He knew how tight money was for people. Thomas appreciated the food he had, but it never compared to the ingenuous gifts he received from the kindhearted folks he met at community food pantries and markets. The young boy's grandmother was one soul he wanted to meet. Christine had followed up with the family and promised to fill him in over dinner.

"Weren't you going to tell me more about that young man and his amazing grandma?" Thomas redirected his daughter to the topic that left him restless at night. It was difficult to sleep well when a child so young was fighting a battle he was too young to understand; yet understood more than the adults who surrounded him.

Chris took another bite. "You know, she uses the food she gets from the pantry, along with collecting the peanut butter and beans from the people who don't use them. She keeps an ongoing pot ready to feed any hungry child or adult with a sort of bean stew." Chris rested her fork on

her plate. "She volunteered in a soup kitchen during her younger days and weeps for the state that Chicago is in. She said she hadn't always lived like that, but she lost her job when the employer moved the operation overseas."

Thomas nodded; he knew the tale well. It was one he'd heard many times before. Manufacturing plants moved out of the country for cheaper labor and fewer restrictions. The employees were often older and had to face ageism when seeking new employment. He had heard the reasoning with vigor by people he met at live events and even in passing; they assumed older folks had no value. That they were unable to learn or work as efficiently as the younger staff. He often interjected with the counterpoint: They were, at times, twenty years younger than many politicians, and the very CEOs of their corporations. He felt it was a copout—a way to avoid the reality that young talent didn't have experience and they did not want to pay for experience.

Thomas preferred to believe that the older people had more to offer society, beyond their so-called prime years. He did not believe in prime as an age—it was a mindset and one that he saw in every phase of adulthood in the people he met during his travels. Some of the older folks he met were filled with untapped ideas, not unlike the grandmother Christine was discussing.

Chris continued talking, "The woman makes peanut butter candy for the kids, and the bean soup over rice is a staple. She keeps the chicken she gets each week for the

boy and his sister. At her age, she has nutritional needs that aren't being met. I doubt she even goes to the doctor."

Thomas pushed his plate away, took his tea mug in two hands, and rested his forehead against the cup. "Let me guess, she also keeps the single loaf of bread to make their sandwiches for school."

"Yup. And since peanut butter isn't allowed, she puts a slice of cheese in them with a bit of mustard. It isn't enough, but they don't ask for more because they know she already has given up her own food for them. For a family of three, they get one chicken, a pound of navy beans, a pound of peanut butter, a pound of cheese, and a can of vegetables. Sometimes she gets sugar, but mostly gets those items when she gets her social security check. She buys flour and mixes it with water to make pancakes and sprinkles sugar on them for the kids. She calls it poor folk food. She does not understand the school lunch program and worries that the state will take her grandchildren away. They are all she has. But she also wants a better life for them." Chris's raised voice caused people at the nearby tables to look her way. "Did you know the video of her grandson running away and you bleeding has gone viral? It's going to ruin their lives. If people wanted to do something, posting a video with no context isn't the way to do it. It's going to garner unwanted attention."

Thomas put his mug on the table. "Do you think she's going to lose them?"

"What? The kids?" Chris sighed. "No, I don't think there's cause. She has food for them, they have beds and

a place to live for now. But if her situation gets worse, the story may change."

The server returned and left the check on the table. Thomas pulled out his wallet to pay. "I hope that video doesn't bring more negative publicity to the high-profile area. It will hurt our cause. The people need the shelter for their safety. It's only humane. I was in New Jersey, a small town off the Palisades Parkway and saw a community garden and thought, if only we could have such a luxury for the people."

"Of course, there would be vandals and the like. Whether we like it or not, crime is real. Sex trafficking is a real problem in this city. Along with theft, burglary, and so on. I'm not being a naysayer, but I am keeping the reality in the dream. I work with the repercussions every day."

"Chris, if dreams stopped because of the what ifs, then what would be the point of dreaming? You can't lose hope. When hope is lost, then what?"

Chris took the last sip of her coffee. "Then I have to have faith. Faith in the people. But my faith is weak. The service sector is struggling. The industry as a whole, is starved. Nearly half of all teachers are lost from burnout, causing them to make career changes. There's a shortage of doctors and nurses, and social workers are in high demand, but not as much as drug abuse and addiction counselors. There is a grave need and people are slow to step up to the challenge. Even the firehouses are declaring their concern."

Thomas put the card in the leather sleeve. "Drug

addiction statistics are staggering. I don't want to go into them, but the growing need for rehab centers and counselors can't be met with the cost of college tuition."

"True," Chris agreed. "The people can't afford the schooling. It's going to get to a point where the existing positions can't be filled because the active professionals are aging out. There isn't anyone to fill their roles and the few that are there, are already stretched thin with caseloads."

Thomas's phone buzzed in his pocket. "Excuse me, cupcake. I have to take this."

Chris nodded.

"Hello?" Thomas said, on his way out of the dining area. He ducked into the empty men's room for privacy.

"Thomas, my man," the excited voice on the other end shouted.

"David? What's up?" Thomas recognized the kind heart and big personality on the other end. They'd crossed paths in the past when the caller gave an anonymous donation to the victims of the California wildfires.

"You are," David said. "You're a rockstar."

Thomas laughed, confused. "You're the rockstar." Then his heart sank deep into his gut. "The video," he whispered.

"Yup. You've gone viral."

Thomas leaned against the cool wall for support. "That really isn't good. That kid was just trying to make a point."

"Hey," David interrupted, "you don't need to tell me. I grew up in his neighborhood. Though the decline is

disheartening, to say the least. It's nothing like I remember it. Tell me what I can do."

Thomas pinched the bridge of his nose. "Right now, I don't actually have an answer. Scholarship money, maybe? But I have to figure out how to stop this impending runaway train wreck."

"Consider it done. Email me what your guidelines are, and I'll make it happen. But you've got me if you think of anything else. I've done a lot for causes. Don't be shy because this hits home. Literally. And I don't like it."

A spark lit in Thomas's chest. He had a scholarship underway, now he needed a bigger, heftier long-term plan. His mind was racing with the possibilities that fundraisers could offer. "Thanks, David. I appreciate it."

"I'll text my manager's number to you, and you just contact him. That number is his personal number. He'll know how to get in contact with me. Talk to you soon, man."

"Will do."

David disconnected the call. Thomas slipped into the men's room. The heat of weariness reddened his skin. The cool water didn't match the dowsing call he just received. The flame of worry was at bay. He just needed to get back to Chris to relay the news.

CHAPTER 6

Golden Dreams

"So, who was it?" Chris asked Thomas when he got back from taking the call.

"An old acquaintance, David Grohl," he said.

"As in, the Foo Fighters?" Chris's voice rose with excitement.

He nodded. David Grohl was a rock star that Thomas had befriended through a benefit over a decade ago. They were sitting at the same table when the singer overheard Thomas talking about how all causes are linked. To donate to one is to donate to many. The problem was finding enough funds to fill all the voids to keep the momentum moving in the right direction. Thomas started at the bottom with individual causes such as scraping together enough funds for medical treatments, libraries, and youth homes. As the price tag grew, so did his need for bodies to fill the vacant positions. Hiring for nonprofits was at an all-time low.

"Let's pick up where we left off. What do you think we need to do to help the situation?"

Christine waited for the waitress to take the bill, sipped her water, and leaned across the table to her father. "Dad, the state jobs are hard because unless you work in the worst rated schools, you don't get a tuition break. The cost of tuition is so much that when a social worker graduates

with a master's and sits for certification, their student loan payments are as much as a mortgage on a small house. And they have this debt following them into the workplace. The average salary of a social worker is around $50,000. After taxes and student loans, they are lucky to net $32,000." She gritted her teeth and sat back against her chair hard, causing her hair to bounce. "You also have to subtract health insurance, life insurance, and retirement. Figure that equals about $8,000. Then you have to run a house on $24,000 a year. And how often do government employees get raises? It's a profession of passion and not for those who want to get rich."

Thomas sat back, thinking about his chat with David Grohl. "I wonder if a scholarship for the specific sectors would garner enough interest to get applicants. Even if we were to do a partial grant, it would help in the long run."

The waitress returned with the processed check. She ventured, "I don't mean to intrude, but I think whatever you're talking about with grants and scholarships is great, but they're really hard to get. They're so competitive, most people don't even try for them."

"Are you in school?" Chris asked.

"I am. Nursing, but I had to settle for an LPN because I can't afford to go to the University to get my bachelor's. I have a toddler at home and live with my mom. Money is tight. I figure I can get a job in Chicago General and put some away for future tuition, but I have to think about my son's future too. I can't sell him short."

Christine frowned and shook her head at her father. "And that's a big part of the problem. Good people want to help, but they aren't afforded a way to do it."

Thomas glanced at the woman and then pulled out his phone. "Young lady, how would you like to continue your education? Give me your information and the name of your school. All I ask is that you get good grades and keep that good heart of yours."

"What?" the waitress screeched. "Are you serious?" Tears rolled down her cheeks. "I don't know what to say."

"Say you'll be a leader in a fading industry," Thomas said.

"Yes, sir. Thank you so much."

"By this time tomorrow, you will have a scholarship covering your costs for the next three years. Consider this an investment in your son's future. He cannot reap if you don't first sow."

The waitress gave Thomas her information while Christine looked on with a smile, the first real smile she had during their intense dinner conversation. It was unexpected at the moment, but not for her father. She knew he was a born giver and knew that each investment he made was in the people; for the people because it was a saying she heard him say repeatedly during her childhood. He wanted her to memorize it and told her so.

When the waitress left, Chris whispered to Thomas, "It's going to take a movement, you know that."

Thomas pushed away from the table and stood, taking

in the breathtaking cityscape that was all Chicago. The Signature Room was located on the ninety-fifth floor, overlooking the streets below. The golden glow of the city lights seemed endless. It was a view unlike any other. In his time, Thomas learned that each city had a heartbeat of its own. It was unique unto its culture, people, and the souls of its founders born into the very core.

Thomas buttoned his suit jacket and pulled his sleeves into place before turning to Chris. "Such a beautiful city under a shroud of darkness."

Christine maneuvered around the table and squeezed her father with a hug. The kind she gave him when she was a child before she learned of the turmoil that existed in the streets below. She realized her father's mission then—but saw it now. She kissed his cheek and whispered, "Chicago needs a superhero, and I think the man chosen is my dad."

#

A week passed since Thomas and Christine's dinner at the Signature Room. In that time, he attended another meeting in the basement of his condominium building. He and Elize were the only residents to attend. Of course, Thomas didn't mind. He enjoyed getting to know people and learning what drove them to be the people they were. This night was no exception. Elize had a range of mini cupcakes and an assortment of green teas set up.

Thomas chose a plain packet and fixed his cup with hot water. He gandered at the sweets and plucked a red

velvet from the tray. "Good evening. And how are you this evening, Ms. Elize?"

Elize giggled, "Oh stop. I'm fine. I suppose I'm not surprised we're the only ones here. After the video of you being struck, I can't say I blame anyone for being leery. It's terrible publicity like that which legitimizes suffering."

"Well, said," he settled his paper cup on a chair beside him and worked to loosen the folds in the miniature morsel. "No son, tonight?"

"Nah," she said, taking a chocolate on chocolate for herself. "He's got to get his homework done. Not time for it tomorrow."

"Oh? Why's that?"

"We go to Lawndale to help at the food pantry where we supply a whole chicken for every family."

"Seriously?" Thomas asked. He set the cupcake on a small napkin she handed him and folded his hands. "You supply an entire community with a chicken—every week?"

Elize blushed, "It's not like they know, besides. People like us can afford fancy cupcakes and fresh cookies. What's a few hundred chickens?"

"Well, well. Do tell what other glorious sides there are to the mysterious Elize," Thomas teased.

"If you must know, the neighborhood committee that involves people from the block meets tomorrow afternoon after the handout. A bunch of us get together and brainstorm ways to help. Each week, we focus on a different aspect of the impoverished sections."

"Is it all people of our stature?"

She shook her head. "Not at all. We have affluent parties and those who just want to feed their neighbors, not willing to acknowledge that they can't feed themselves."

Intrigued by the opportunity before him, Thomas couldn't resist tagging along if Elize did not see him as an imposition. "Would you mind a guest on your quest tomorrow?"

"If you're asking to come along, we'd be delighted. There hasn't been a new face at the pantry in some time. It's like the few of us who show what the other community members think should be adequate for voluntary service. The only ones who come through are mandated by the magistrate for community service."

"They probably need help as much as the folks they serve."

"You understand well, Mr. Thomas."

#

The meeting hall was packed when Thomas and Elize arrived. A woman he recognized from a real estate billboard was siting in the front row. Thomas took the seat behind her. Elize left him to go sit by several members of their condo complex who came to support the measure. It was voting night and more people filled the public space than had at the previous meeting.

Board members filed in, took their seats, and the proceedings began. Thomas had brought a wealth of

knowledge with him. He memorized it all from times past. It didn't matter what city, they all needed help in the common arena of public need. The woman from the billboard raised her hand. The board granted her the podium.

"It is my intention to bring opportunity to the people in the North Lawndale community. They need more than homeless shelters and food pantries. These people have no clothes to compete in job interviews. The truth is that one of the biggest issues facing low-income neighborhoods is the lack of Wi-Fi. A lot of times computers and laptops needed to write resumes are irrelevant because they have no internet access at home. And there is no easy transportation to get to a public facility with Wi-Fi access. I actually think the dilapidated structure on the border of Near Westside would serve a multitude of worthwhile purposes. The shelter could be an extended arrangement for thirty to ninety days. The bottom floor would consist of a shop with clothes, suits, free toiletries, and basic computer facilities equipped with free Wi-Fi. There would also be personal assistance for those who don't know how to navigate basic technology."

A roar rumbled through the jammed enclosure. The chairman brought down the gavel, causing the commotion to hush.

"A shelter, here in Near Westside? I think not," the angry woman from the previous meeting said. Her daughter sat beside her, staring at the floor. "Unemployment and homelessness do not need to go hand in hand. I have no problem with supporting people and giving them an

opportunity to succeed, but I do have a problem with introducing criminal activity and vagrants."

This time, a louder wave of deep voices overrode the sound of the gavel. An older woman near the end of the front table stood, whistling to get the angered community members' attention. "People, please. Nothing will be accomplished with outbursts and interruptions. If you have something to say, the place is at the podium."

Again, the room fell silent. The real estate agent closed her file. "Thank you."

It was Thomas's turn to take to the floor. He approached the podium, grasped the top, and leaned toward the people.

"My name is Thomas Matthews. Perhaps some of you have heard of me, perhaps not. I am the victim of the vicious pebble video." Nervous laughter dotted the audience. "To tell the truth, I am worried." He stepped out from behind the wooden podium. "Chicago is a city that was founded in 1833. That's nearly two hundred years ago. Think about that." He paused and walked behind the stand, giving the attendees an opportunity to absorb his words. "After the inception of the railroad, it became a bustling city. A city that promised new opportunities to immigrants, the grain industry, and railroads. Four decades later, disaster struck. The Chicago Fire devastated the city. Nearly one third was lost, claiming nearly three hundred lives. It left one hundred thousand people homeless."

He stood back and scanned the faces in the audience. He could have heard a pin drop in the silence. It was his

gift. Thomas was a natural born storyteller who was known for telling the best stories in a way that nobody else could. "Think about that. The first homeless problem was created by unsafe business practices, an inadequate infrastructure, and a city that did not provide for those left suffering. They were displaced mothers and fathers, daughters, and sons. And at that time, many were illiterate, unable to read a job application, or understand their rights. Though I guess one grace was the erection of the first skyscraper which housed a ten-story insurance building. Ironic."

He left the floor to sit back in his metal chair. The real estate agent applauded. Soon the entire room was filled with quizzical faces that applauded while murmuring to their neighbors. Thomas could hear the comments:

"The idea is great, but."

"Well, I don't see why it has to be so close. Can't it go further into North Lawndale?"

"I think it's great."

"Me too. I try to help when I can."

"I've heard of these places. I feel so bad for the people."

"I'm not a sympathizer when it comes to my kids. Safe is what matters."

"You don't think they want to be safe?"

The voices arose to a level that drowned out all the other noise. Thomas wanted the people to think. He wanted to give them an alternative outlook to the stereotype. The kind of business he described was one that had proven effective and turned many families back into mainstream society. It

was never as easy as he heard people say, "Go get a job." It was a common phrase thrown toward those on the streets. But getting a job was not so easy.

He knew people often had no documentation—no birth certificates and sometimes they had no means to get to the place where they were born. They had no clean clothes, appropriate attire for an interview or first pay period. They didn't have the money for security on an apartment or money for utilities. Mental health services were lacking in a community wrought with unaddressed mental health issues. Childcare and transportation were other real concerns.

The people needed security, and Thomas wanted to give them the means to make it so. He felt reassured by the real estate woman and Elize. The board members did not show a hint as to what side they were leaning. It was a safe bet that they would discuss the points before putting in their votes and declaring the decision. Though Thomas knew he could appeal the decision, he did not believe he would have to. The board members and attendees were quick to show raised tempers. The scene reminded Thomas of the time he was raising funds for an ongoing literacy project. The townspeople did not see the need when the local community college was declaring the urgency. It was a merry-go-round of meetings, speeches, and votes.

The chairperson led the board out of the room to a corner office they used for the monthly meetings. It was merely a space with a desk and three chairs. Thomas was

going to slip to the hall and take in a moment of silence in a room adjacent to the one they would use, but Patricia made her way back to the podium.

"People please," she shouted.

A hush came over the crowd as they realized she was poised to speak.

"Let the voting take place before we bring forth arguments that have no need baring."

Thomas was impressed with her ability to bring order to the mayhem. He also enjoyed her verbiage. He liked a good turn of phrase and gave credit where it was due. When she stepped away, the chairperson hit the gavel. "We've reached a decision."

CHAPTER 7

Remembrance

The room was silent. Each resident focused on the front table. Some with crossed arms, others with hunched shoulders and pained faces. Patricia stared straight ahead as did the real estate agent who presented the idea for a full circle shelter. Thomas folded his hands. With the commotion moments before, he wasn't sure which way the board would sway.

"The decision is sixty forty in favor of seeking an alternative building for the shelter. This meeting is adjourned."

Thomas sunk back in his seat. The motion failed.

Elize hugged him. "There's always next month. We can appeal and see what happens. Perhaps we can come better prepared."

"I was hoping it wouldn't come to that, but it is what it is. I'm just thankful it wasn't a unanimous decision. Two votes and we win," Thomas urged. "There is good in the hearts of all these folks. We just have to get them to open up their minds to match them."

Elize shrugged, "I guess. But I'm tired and just want to go home and relax. Maybe pour a nice glass of Pinot and take in the city lights from my balcony."

"That sounds nice, Elize. You have a good evening." Thomas gave her a folded lip smile and retreated into the

crowd. Whenever a vote didn't go his way, he tended to start the analysis of what went wrong. He truly believed that every obstacle had a means of conquering it. He just had to be smart enough to find a way.

#

A week later, Thomas, Elize, and the other residents in the condo complex met for their regular evening event. This time, Thomas was prepared with a nonprofit plan that would not fail. He had the know-how and the expertise. He just needed to put it to work while engaging the assistance of those who shared a similar passion.

"Good evening," he said. "Tonight is about refocusing and regrouping. At the end of this meeting, we are going to have a working business plan. I believe it was the downfall of our stance, and one that cannot be overlooked. Every good idea needs structure to succeed."

Elize sipped her coffee as she stared at the booklet Thomas had laid before them. "Where do we start?"

Thomas picked up a template he printed for a nonprofit business plan. "First, we need to address the community's needs. How will they benefit most?"

One young man spoke up. "We need to learn how to build a library to promote literacy programs. I remember you talking about people not knowing how to fill out a job application or perform a job search."

"Excellent point!" Thomas said, writing the word 'literacy.'

Elize raised a finger. "Food pantry with shelves for ethnic diversity."

Thomas wrote that down as well. "And I'm going to add shelter."

"I don't think we need the clothes as much because of all the thrift shops and Goodwill stores around. The basic needs are most important," the young man added.

"Well, let's write it just for reference." Thomas added interview clothing, leaving room for more suggestions as the night grew on. "Now, let's discuss our mission statement. It has to reflect our long-term goals. I think we all want the same short term."

Elize pitched in, "I think short term is to get the homeless off the street and fed. Long term is giving them the tools they need to stay off the streets."

Thomas wrote those down next. "So, what is a good statement?"

Elize's son raised his hand. "What about inspiring communities to invest in themselves for a better tomorrow?"

"I like that," the others said.

Thomas wrote it down. "This is going faster than I thought. So, who wants to be the officers?"

The young man chimed in, "I think Elize should be the President because she's been fighting for this for a while. And Thomas should be the Vice President."

Thomas put up his hands. "I am flattered by the suggestion, but I have so many roles already. I would love to be a member and take part in meetings, but I think an officer's

role is a permanent position. That belongs to someone who has a more traditional lifestyle and won't go jetting off to give lectures. Why not you, young man?"

"You're always trying to help, and you have great ideas," Elize said.

The young man looked at the other members, who gave him a thumbs up. "Okay, I accept."

"Great, then will the rest of you take treasurer and secretary?"

After all agreed to the positions, Elize wrote the minutes declaring who was assigned to each role. All those with a title signed the paper. "We have to open an account, but I think we need more than this document for our vision."

"True," Thomas agreed. "First, we need to find a new space for the shelter and then get a lawyer because we need to file Articles of Incorporation for a nonprofit and look into a 501c3 so our purchases will be tax exempt."

"We also need to do a fundraiser and food drive," a young woman who agreed to be treasurer said. "If we want this model to work, then we have to find a way to keep it going regardless of officer status. I mean, we can't keep funding the shelter. There has to be a budget and some sort of monies."

The group continued to discuss the details and plan where to search for the structure that would carry out their mission. "I'll reach out to that real estate agent who was at the meeting. If she can find us a building in North Lawndale, we will probably gain the extra two votes necessary

to pass the motion," Elize offered. "I'm not even sure we really need the support of the board at that point, but it's a formality because we started the process."

"Good thinking," Thomas said.

#

The following weekend, Christine caught up with Thomas. He was on his way to join her and the kids for dinner. In the week after the motion failed, they spoke about the community's needs and lack of support. Thomas decided to expand his vision. Thomas had always been passionate about helping those in need. He had volunteered at various soup kitchens and homeless shelters throughout his life, but he had always wanted to do more. Thomas also spoke with the agent about a prime opportunity. Later, he took a detour before dinner to scope out the location. When he saw the dilapidated brick building on Harding Avenue, he knew it was their chance to make a difference.

The building had been abandoned for years, and the windows were boarded up with plywood. The brickwork was crumbling and the roof had several large holes. But Thomas saw the potential in the building. It was large enough to house a significant number of people, and the location was perfect for a homeless shelter. The bottom floor would be large enough for the food pantry and small thrift shop, but he wanted to add to their agenda. Christine had mentioned mental health and a walk-in clinic. He wanted to overcome one hurdle at a time, but planned to

approach the condo committee with an expanded vision. One that served all ages and abilities. Even if they couldn't house them or feed them, perhaps they would provide the much-needed care Christine insisted they needed.

"Dad," she had said, "these people need a safe space, and I don't mean to sleep. They need to feel confident going for help. You should consider adding a counseling center or an abuse hotline. Something where troubled teens could escape to, or addicts could come in to straighten out. What about kids, teens, and adults that just need a mentor to guide them out of poverty? They don't need to stay there; they need a beacon of hope. You said you wanted full circle. Well, I give you full circle."

Thomas was so impressed by his daughter's words of wisdom that he couldn't suppress the excitement. He presented the idea when he attended the next committee meeting. They didn't waste any time. Thomas contacted the real estate agent, and within a week, he had approval from Elize and the other committee officers to acquire the building. They celebrated the purchase over a champagne toast in the meeting room.

"Now that we are the proud owners of," Elize paused, "What shall we call it?"

"How about the Hope Center?" the young man offered.

"We can try, but I bet it's taken," said the treasurer. "How about Full Circle?"

The committee agreed. They also agreed to reach out to their friends and family, asking for their support. "We

have a team of people who share their passions for helping others. Now it's time to put the word out to all those in favor at the community hall," the young man stated.

It wasn't long before they had a group of dedicated volunteers ready to help them transform the building into a full circle shelter. The young man had a handful of blind investors while Elize put up her own funds, as did Thomas. It was Elize's son who came up with the idea of collaborating with the local soup kitchens to spread the word. Thomas brought Christine to see the property in North Lawndale. The structure was majestic in its architecture, though a quick glancing passerby would hesitate to agree. Of that, he was certain. It was a six-story brick building with a rusted fire escape and several broken windows on the first floor. The entrance floor's hardwood floors needed refinishing, as there were digs in the wood, but overall, with minimal investment, it would be ready to go. The major concerns were the graffiti covered sheetrock walls that had large holes, garbage from squatters, and drug paraphernalia left behind.

Each room would become an efficiency that would house four beds. There were twenty-four apartments in total. That meant twenty-four bathrooms and kitchens that needed to be renovated or removed to allow for higher occupancy for quality of life. The quality of life was an important factor when working with the homeless, Thomas learned from experience.

Quality of life meant hitting the basic human needs.

People wanted to feel safe. Safe from the elements, safe from crime, and safe from the psychological abuse that came from discerning residents. Thomas understood the homeless came from executive positions in the corporate world, teens escaping abusive homes, and veterans unable to adapt to civilian life. He also understood that many were reclusive alcoholics and addicts to various narcotics, opioids, and whatever new substance was rotating through the street supplier's circuit.

The street suppliers were often pushers who had ties to larger gangs. These gangs answered to the cartels and whoever was in charge of their specific ring. But when it came down to it, the drugs were smuggled in, and pushers were responsible for getting clients hooked. The homeless people were someone's grandmothers, mothers, sisters, grandfathers, fathers, or sons. Some were aunts and others were uncles. Some were driven to the streets because of their familial disputes over beliefs and personal identification. None of them chose to live in filth or to go into prostitution, which was part of the human trafficking ring.

Two of the newest addictives were nitazene and xylazine. Thomas saw synthetic marijuana take the lives of young mothers. Fentanyl was another illicit drug responsible for taking the lives of those who purchased heroin and cocaine laced with the lethal drug. It was one of the reasons Thomas had to keep up to date on his Narcan training and also through disaster preparation programs. He knew he needed to have a mental tool-belt that let him

have the knowledge and the ability to combat the addiction epidemic from a responder's side.

Realistically, he and all the medical personnel he worked with knew the only ones who possessed an insider's view were those who were recovering addicts from any or all of the illegal substances.

Heroin and opioids were the two most common in the news.

It was Thomas's understanding that people heard about them but didn't know what they were, how they affected people, or even what it involved. Most people thought a prescription was all that was needed for the latter. But heroin was a whole other ball game.

Heroin was a process. It involved mixing and shooting into a vein. One would have to buy needles and find a place to inject them that wouldn't draw suspicion. Thomas heard the story many times. For some reason, heroin was the drug that scared many addicts into using the cheaper street substances.

Ecstasy was another psychologically addictive street drug. Thomas knew that some people considered it a gateway drug because it seemed harmless. In fact, he knew a first-year student at Chicago University who wanted to try ecstasy in the worst way. He met the kid, just nineteen years old, during a food drive. Thomas thought he had a bright future.

Stepping into the new building, Thomas thought about Sean.

The eager student hoisted himself with ease into the back of the panel truck. From Thomas's inquisition, he learned that the young man was a communications major. "Good day, young sir," Thomas called to him.

"Hi, I'm Sean. I'm with the Honor's Program."

Thomas put his hand out. "Nice to meet you."

Sean shook his hand. "Likewise."

"That's a firm grip you've got there."

The boy smiled. "Thanks, I used to play varsity football."

The next time Thomas saw him, was at a school production of *Taming of the Shrew* by William Shakespeare, seven months later. He liked to support the arts as much as the sports because he realized the world needed a variety of talent. Music, acting, painting, and sporting events were part of life around the globe. He was impressed by Sean's acting skills.

After the show, Thomas waited for him in the theater's lobby. When he saw the boy's red curly haired six-foot seven-inch frame back in the truck, he realized he was looking at an athlete. Less than a year later, some of the muscle became lean. He was all smiles when Thomas called out to him. "Sean!"

Sean stopped, looked in the direction of Thomas's voice, and scampered over. A smile spread across his face. "Mr. Thomas! I wouldn't expect you to come here, of all places. Then again, I guess so because you are such a supportive person."

Thomas smiled back. "You were fantastic. You could have a new career before you."

"Yeah, but my heart's not in it." Sean glanced at a group of girls that huddled past him, giggling. "It was great of you to come. Maybe I'll see you again sometime."

Thomas nodded.

Little did he know how or when.

A year passed when he flew in from Tulsa. Thomas was asked to give a graduation speech. He was to address the students with sage advice for their changing futures and how the power to change the world was in their hands. The only thing standing in their way was themselves. From the stage he saw the EMT's go by. After the ceremony, he inquired at the security office about the happenings.

They directed him to Chicago General Hospital.

Once there, he knew. The red-haired Sean was in the emergency room, barely conscious from an asthma attack. "What happened?"

Sean rolled his eyes toward Thomas. "Hey."

Thomas waited for him to speak. He noted his physical appearance. The lack of muscle tone, sunken cheeks, black circles beneath the eyes. His hair was thin and lackluster. "What'd you take?" he asked, not giving the now twenty-year-old a chance to avoid him.

"Crank."

Thomas's chest tightened. He knew what that did—methamphetamine tore lives from their captives. And that is exactly what he considered those addicted to

meth—prisoners of the substance. "Tell me how you got to this point, Sean." He wanted an open-ended question because a yes or no was too easy. Thomas knew that battling an epidemic meant getting to the cause.

"I'm not sorry," Sean whispered.

"I didn't ask you to be. I just want to know what the allure was. Consider me curious."

"That night after the play, I went with the girls, and I tried ecstasy. I know a lot of people who take it and I wanted to. It wasn't pushed on me. I wanted to experience it, and I loved it. It made every piece of my body hyper aware."

Thomas nodded in affirmation. "You wanted to chase the high because it was that good."

"Yeah, I guess. I mean, I smoked weed, but that was nothing. I wasn't about to do heroin. I didn't want the needles and lines. But Monster was easy."

"You mean crack or powdered cocaine?"

"Powdered at first. I got it free, just had to go to parties where they were setting out lines. They'd be there handing out straws like they were party favors."

Thomas sighed. "I bet they did. But that's a high society crowd. They don't do meth, at least, not usually. How did you get here, Sean?"

"Crack." He swallowed. "I didn't come from an affluent family. I was at the university on my parent's life savings and my dad cashed out his 401k. Those people could buy it when they wanted. Some kept it in the freezer of their mini

fridges. I couldn't afford it and this guy at one of the parties offered me a smoke."

"And you accepted," Thomas finished.

Sean's eyes misted, then he coughed. Blood sprinkled the tissue he'd used to cover his mouth. "I'm bleeding!"

"Meth can do that, Sean. I'll get the nurse. Sometimes we need to reach rock bottom before deciding we want to change our paths. Just think about it. You are a young, healthy man. You have your whole life…"

"Ahem," a female doctor about Thomas's age interrupted his spiel. "Sean, how ya feeling?"

"Not so good." He showed her the tissue.

"Do I have your permission to speak in front of this gentleman?" She pointed to Thomas.

Sean coughed out an affirmative reply. "Yes."

"Well, I looked over the report to your CT scan and x-rays. The blood you're seeing isn't from the meth directly."

Sean let out a sigh.

"We believe it is lung cancer. We need to do a biopsy to confirm and a full body scan to make sure it hasn't spread."

Thomas instinctively grabbed Sean's hand.

#

Christine put her hand on Thomas's shoulder. He was deep in his memories when she brought him to the present. It reminded him that he should reach out to the young lad who was now in his thirties. "Penny for your thoughts?"

"This place reminds me of a kid, well, a young man that I know. I thought I found him at rock bottom when he learned he had lung cancer, but actually his bottom was in an abandoned building, not unlike this."

"Did he overdose?" she asked.

"No," Thomas smiled. "He had undergone several surgeries related to the cancer. He lost one lung and had a few lesions removed from his brain. The treatment left him with subtle brain damage and hearing loss, but they cured the cancer after eight years."

"Wow, that's horrific and amazing at the same time. I mean, medicine has advanced so much, but it's so sad that he had to go through all that."

"Yup. But Sean didn't let it stop him. He finished a drug and alcohol abuse counseling certification program and goes into crack houses, reaching out to those who've nowhere to go but up."

Christine shook her head. "Incredible. He's a good man. I'm glad he's out there making a difference. Everyone needs a bucket of chances."

Thomas squeezed her hand. "You can say that again."

CHAPTER 8

Voices

Over the years, Thomas knew other shelters that continued to grow. But when he met with Elize, his desire was to make a new model. One that would develop and grow with unforeseen needs. He met with the committee over dinner where they discussed adding even more services and programs. Their mission was to help thousands, if not countless, people get back on their feet.

As he had told Elize that night, when she had told him to be proud of his accomplishments, "How can I be proud when the reality is that I've only scratched the surface? There are people who won't live through the night around the world, and it will be because of one of the issues we dared address in the last attempt to sway the community. Starvation and hypothermia are real. Crimes against humankind are at a disgusting high, and most do not have a place they can check into."

"Thomas, we knew that buying that dilapidated brick building was a gamble. We know it has the potential to impact this community on a level they can't fathom. We will succeed at the upcoming meeting," Elize said.

Thomas smiled, "And if we are met with opposition, we will not back away. We will fight harder because the people need a positive change."

The treasurer sipped her coffee. "Listen, I learned so much along the way, I can't express to what extent. And I don't just mean about the construction and management, but about compassion, empathy, and the power of community. All these people need to do is walk through an existing shelter. They'll understand their purpose. I may spend the rest of my life following in your footsteps. Personally, I've never felt as necessary as I do now."

The young man offered his own take away from their collaboration. "Even as I look to the future and understand that there is still so much work to be done, I feel empowered to take on more. Homelessness should not be the epidemic it is. We, as wealthy members of society, have the means to make a difference, but as people, we can forge the way just as you have shown. We get our hands dirty. We put on our work clothes and start the demolition. I took part in planting tomato plants in the vacant lot next door. Even if people don't have our money, they can make a difference."

Thomas nodded, "Exactly. They need to learn to help themselves and take charge because all too often we see they suffer because no one else will."

As the group left the restaurant for the night, Thomas paused to take in the buildings that surrounded them. Chicago was a city with history. A history that he hoped was still growing and one that would make this city set an example for the rest of the world. He understood that the neglected buildings were hopeful buildings, and vacant lots had the potential to feed a neighborhood. It was all in

the vision. The eye of the beholder, as the saying went. He felt hope in his bones and knew that his excitement would reach the board members. Because he knew his only choice was to win the fight. It was his determination that lit the fire in his neighbor's hearts, and the act was infectious. He just needed to make the other residents see.

"You're a dreamer, you know that?" Elize said.

"If it wasn't for dreams, where would any of us be? We are the results of someone's future. Their dreams; their goals."

#

The evening of the meeting arrived. Thomas and Elize were the only ones available. They decided to meet outside the town hall building. They had the plans, blueprints, and all the documentation they thought they would need. Thomas had taken pictures in preparation of any protests that might happen at the location. It was further from the border, and therefore, offered a better opportunity for the extra votes.

"Ready to rustle some feathers?" he teased when she walked up to him on the sidewalk. There had already been several protesters holding signs. Most were against the idea. "I know I am."

"Sure am. We really need this second chance."

Thomas raised his brow at her. "Speaking of chances and change, are you ready to face the plethora of screaming, oh sorry, protesting residents?"

"No," Elize chided. "But when did that ever stop us?"

#

Thomas and Elize took their seats in the middle of the rows of metal folding chairs. More people were in attendance than the last. Thomas knew it was most likely the viral video that brought the two sides together for an angry outburst. To his surprise, the protesters had brought signs into the room. He sat in an aisle seat on the side that was primarily for the shelter.

Patricia and her daughter Mary were there. They sat on the opposite side and stared straight ahead, avoiding Thomas and Elize whenever they glanced their way. Thomas took note because he knew there was guilt or shame that drove her to do so. In his experience, he needed to find the crack in her armor to get inside and learn why she had the opinions that she did. He knew everyone had a reason, but that did not mean they knew how to convey it.

"Hello, Patricia," Thomas said. He waved at her daughter, Mary, who waved back before huddling into her mother.

"Thomas," Patricia acknowledged.

He noticed a bound packet in her hands. "Are you going to present tonight?"

She nodded her head, "If time permits."

"I look forward to hearing your points." He smiled.

She squinted at him, then turned to face the front.

The board took their seats at the front table. Opening

statements were given, as were a reading of the last meetings happenings by the secretary. Patricia was chosen to go first to the podium.

"Good evening, everyone." Patricia opened her report. "Let me start by saying, the last meeting is proof why I am against bringing a shelter to this community. I want to point out that property values will decrease more than they would with any other type of entity, be it a crematorium or hospital. We as real estate investors, that's what we are if we own property, have a right to say what we do and do not approve of. Homeless shelters have proven to bring in illicit drugs, addicted individuals, and prostitution."

Several people stood on Thomas's side of the room. "That's not true. It's stereotypical dribble." They hollered at Patricia.

Her face flustered. "No, that kid attacked a peaceful protest and struck an innocent bystander. Where was his grandmother? A kid that young should not be running the streets. If vagrants come in, then what? More violence. Fights, filth, and vandalism will rise. Problems surround these structures. And they also happen inside halfway houses and shelters. What happens when there aren't enough beds? They start camping on the streets. I, for one, fear for my daughter if these people move to the North Lawndale structure. It's a cost we as a community cannot afford. We have little to no crime in our neighborhood, and I want to keep it that way." She closed her report, swiped it from the podium, and marched toward her seat.

The people on Thomas's side were yelling and counter arguments were verbally thrust toward one another. Patricia grabbed her daughter Mary's wrist and pulled her after her from the row. She pushed through the standing room only crowd and rushed out of the community room doors.

Thomas was instantly concerned for her safety and leapt from his seat. He exited the room behind her.

CHAPTER 9

Trepidation

homas was bewildered by Patricia's flustered state. After she said her piece, she rushed her daughter, Mary, down the row of metal chairs, toward the exit. She was one of the ones who wanted to emphasize one side of the perception rather than hold an objective approach to the panoramic view presented when all sides were finished presenting. Thomas understood her points and believed they were true, but invalid.

All too often, property values were used as bargaining chips or dissuasions to stress a cause. It was a transference of knowledge. One that said the one with the most money or power ruled the room with respect because it was just the way society structured the general belief system. Thomas knew it well. The man in the suit got the deal, not because he was the best, but because he looked the part. Just like the neighborhoods with the lower incomes tended to have more social facilities with programs for the general public, including halfway houses and shelters.

Thomas knew there needed to be an awakening. One that showed the value of community enrichment to all parties. He just wasn't sure how to accomplish the task. It was clear to him the woman who rushed her daughter from the room was upset and angry after the community board refused to listen to her concerns. He knew they were not

only her concerns, but also the concerns of all the protesters who had gathered at prior meetings. He was almost certain they were the concerns of Chicago's real estate agents, too.

He knew that shelters brought home values down between ten and fifteen percent. That was less than cemeteries and the same as garbage dumps. It sickened him when he thought about the human factor being worth less alive than deceased.

He thought to himself, *If only they could glimpse the smile on a mother's face when she was granted a bed for her and her children. Or to watch a shivering youth huddle into a gray government issued blanket as if it were a parcel of luxury.* But that was the problem, he knew. People did not understand luxury. It was not a name brand purse, but warmth, and a blanket to pull up to one's chin. The feel of a warm mug in the hands of a hypothermic veteran, or the security of a brick building to a woman fleeing her husband's fist for leaving.

Thomas hurried to catch up to Patricia with several men and women on his heels. Whether or not the meeting was adjourned, he did not know. He wanted to reach the woman and her daughter to talk in private. The last thing he wanted to do was invalidate her concerns. Conflict would not win any points for either side of the argument. Compromise and mediation were Thomas's tools for gaining ground in what seemed to be a losing battle. More often than not, he opened hearts by appealing to the mind.

As Thomas hurried down the stairs, he heard the

others filling the well above him. He glimpsed Patricia a few yards ahead of him. She dashed through the metal door. Thomas leapt to the door before it closed. With over fifty community residents in the meeting, he wanted to get outside before there was a conflict on the street. But when he got to the sidewalk, the sight before him made his heart seize in his chest.

A white van covered in graffiti was parked at the curb. A tall Caucasian man in a black ski hat, white hoodie, and faded denim jeans lunged from the front door. His focus was on another man. One dressed from head to toe in black with Mary's arms in his grip.

"Mary," Patricia screamed, "no!"

Thomas saw the fear in Mary as her body tensed; paralyzed. The man drug her to the open sliding door where yet another counterpart in black awaited. He motioned with his hand for the one struggling with the child to hurry.

Patricia had slung her purse at them, but they were faster. The man in the hoodie scooped Mary's feet out from under her and secured her legs in his arms. She tried to kick, but they were moving her to the van.

Thomas ran, his voice breaking as he hollered, "Let her go!"

Before he had time to react, a figure appeared from the shadows. It darted toward the men. When he neared the kidnappers, he ducked and charged with his shoulder, then rolled to the ground and grabbed the one with Mary's upper body. He wrapped his legs around the man's legs,

knocking him off balance. The guy in the white hoodie dropped her legs and took off on foot down the sidewalk.

"Stop him!" someone yelled from behind Thomas.

A group of men took off after him. Two young men darted after him. The adrenaline pulsing in the air pressed in. The men reached the fleeing man. They tackled him, his face hitting the road. One sat on the guy's back, pulling his arm behind him. The other demanded he stay put.

"Don't move. I swear to you, don't freaking move."

The driver of the van started the vehicle and drove off before anyone could stop them, but the anonymous figure from the shadows kept the man, who initially snatched Mary, in his grasp and pinned him to the curb. The girl's savior twisted his legs, forcing the perpetrator to lie face down on the pavement.

Free from the attacker's hands, Mary ran to her mother. "Mommy," she cried. Sobs bubbled from her throat when she took a breath. An inaudible string of words got swallowed by her frantic tears.

Patricia ran to meet her, flinging her shoes from her feet. "Oh, my baby girl." The mother and daughter collapsed on the walkway where the crowd of folks from the meeting were streaming from the small metal doorway. Thomas squatted next to Patricia and patted her shoulder. The woman pulled her daughter to her chest and hugged Thomas.

A tattered camouflage duffle bag lay on the concrete just out of the alley's shadows. "It's that homeless guy,"

someone called while picking up his bag. "That guy over there saved her."

Thomas went to the hero to offer his assistance. He understood a citizen's arrest was legal in the instance of a bystander intervening in an attack or crime in progress. He also knew that the individual who intervened could use force to stop the criminal act. It concerned him, because he saw how hard the man struck the other. He didn't want a good deed to turn into an extreme situation—one where the homeless man was arrested for a crime he didn't intend to commit.

"Want me to take over?" Thomas asked.

"No, I've got this. You go make sure they're okay. I think they'd feel safer if you were to check on them. I'm not exactly the face of safety they want to see." The homeless man shook a lock of hair from his eyes. "Did someone call 9-1-1 yet?"

"Already on it," a female onlooker said. "You're a hero."

He ducked his head between his elbows, wiping sweat from his brow. "The girl got away. That's all that matters."

"Nonsense. Most people would run away or stand and watch. You acted, and that is an act of heroism. I'm sure those men had guns, but you went in there without hesitation. Fear can cause cowardice, but you seemed to have none."

The man raised a shoulder. "Chicago is a hub for human trafficking, primarily for children and women. It was never a question of the men's intentions. I knew the moment I

saw them what they wanted. If she hadn't been walking ahead of her mother, they might not have had a chance to grab her. Though they may have gotten both the mother and child if that older gentleman or I hadn't been here." He repositioned himself to talk to the growing crowd. "Almost twenty thousand women and children are thought to be victims of traffickers."

"I didn't know it was such an issue. You don't really hear about it on the news. I mean, once in a while they mention something, but you'd have to have a kidnapping every day to reach the numbers you state," the woman from the crowd said. "What even is human trafficking? No one ever explains it."

Thomas was halfway between the fellow on the ground and Patricia. "Let me answer that," he said. "Human trafficking is a term for the capture and enforcement of illicit acts on another human by either families or strangers. Often, these acts are for sexual purposes. Money is exchanged for the individual in a sale, or for a service. No matter what the purpose, this industry is in the top three for criminal practices on a global scale. These transactions occur across the country and often cross paths with the drug and smuggling trade."

The woman pulled her sweater around her arms. "I'll never understand why people even get started doing stuff like that."

"Money," the homeless man said.

"It always comes to money," another woman said.

"What happened to helping your fellow man, and the golden rule?"

The young man glanced at Thomas. "When it comes to helping, a lot of times, people think about how it will affect them. Will they benefit and how? If it has a negative impact, either tangible or not, then they are less likely to put forth the work and effort."

"Mommy," Mary said, making the crowd focus on her. "I want to go home."

Patricia's hands shook as she pulled her daughter into her lap on the sidewalk. "We have to talk to the police officers when they get here. When they tell us we can go, I'll take you straight home and fix you a nice bath."

"No, Mommy. I don't want to be alone."

Patricia kissed her forehead. "I don't plan on leaving you alone for a long time."

"Not ever." Mary pressed into her mother. "I don't want to go to school tomorrow."

One woman in the crowd offered advice to Patricia. "When a trauma happens, the school psychologist and guidance counselors can help. Just call the office and they will talk to you and your daughter. Things like this are hard to make into reality and replay themselves. It has the potential to fester if not addressed. The counselors in Chicago are phenomenal. I know because my sister was trafficked." The woman stepped toward the middle. "We got her back after the FBI located her three months into her disappearance. She was abducted in Chicago and found in

Albuquerque, New Mexico. As we know, this is an issue in cities like New York, St. Louis, and Baton Rouge. But it's actually an issue in all cities, not just major ones. It's in our backyards and we don't even realize it."

Patricia bit her lip as it trembled. "I could have lost my baby forever."

"Don't say that," Thomas said, rushing toward her. "You can't focus on the things that could have happened. If that was the case, then we, as humans, would never leave our homes. We would be bound. That is why we have friends and family to help. Patricia, do you have someone for you and Mary?" Thomas stepped toward her slowly. He saw she was in shock and not the mental state to reason.

"Mary's all I have. She's my world. Do you know the awful things they could have done to her? Where she would have ended up? How she could have ended up? How am I supposed to live with the knowledge of the horrors that almost hit within my own walls?"

Thomas knew she needed time to process what happened. Panic was setting in for Patricia and she needed to get through the could-haves in order to see what really did happen. But he knew, all too well, that panic and runaway imaginations were harbingers of incomprehension and the inability to reason. Patricia was at that point, and he wanted to keep her from sinking any further into the abyss.

CHAPTER 10

Reciprocity

"**M**ary, I've got you both," Thomas said. He pulled the shaking girl and her mother, Patricia, into his arms.

Mary's eyes sparkled, a reflection from the floodlight outside the town hall. Patricia reached for her daughter, folding her arms around the girl, who broke into sobs. Thomas remained by their sides. The young girl cried into her mother's shoulder.

"If that man hadn't been here," the girl gasped.

"I know, baby. I love you so much." Mary squeezed her daughter and stepped back from Thomas. "I owe you an apology."

"It isn't me who was hurt by the debate." Thomas pointed to the young man squatting behind the attacker who he had secured. He had the assailant's arm secured to his back, making sure he remained seated on the curb. "Sometimes we are too quick to judge. Just because someone is homeless doesn't mean they are the criminals."

The crowd of emotionally charged community residents emerged from the building. Patricia and Mary stood close to Thomas as five men ran toward the homeless man. "Don't. He saved my little girl!" she hollered, but the mob was too loud to hear her words.

They looked at the homeless man, whispering and pointing. A circle formed around him and the five men pulling at his shoulders. He tried to shake them off and lost his grip on the kidnapper. He didn't let it keep him from losing his charge. Instead, he wrapped a leg around him and locked his ankles.

Thomas's voice boomed over the ruckus. "Enough." Several people turned their heads to look at him. "That man is a hero. He saved this innocent child from the man on the ground, and you are proving the point of negative profiling."

The chairman from the meeting pushed through the mass of people. Thomas joined her, worried about the homeless man's well-being. The last thing he wanted was to let the wrong man go. Thomas had witnessed the pent-up anger that escalated good meaning people's emotions to the point where they could not be reasoned with. The innocent party often ended up hurt, and in one instance, dead. He wanted to prevent that from happening. He used his voice and shoved his way through the crowd to get to the homeless man, who was pleading with the men surrounding him.

The chairman reached the curb first. "Excuse me," the chairman said to the young man.

The young man peered up at him. His tangled hair blew in the chill summer breeze. He kept his grip on the trafficker, readjusting his balance by putting a knee to the ground. "Yes, sir?"

Thomas rushed to squat beside him. "Listen to me," he yelled, "All too often an intentional move causes a rush to judgement. Too many times I have witnessed a misinterpreted good deed. You must remain calm." He raised his hands, palms facing the crowd. "This man is a genuine hero, and you are denying him the right to explain himself." He turned to the young man. "Where did you learn to tackle like that?" Thomas knew the young man's statement would clarify his position in the situation, appeasing the assuming crowd. Thomas nodded at the five men who stepped back. Take this man on the ground and keep him until the police arrive."

The confused five men grappled with the detainee on the ground, getting him to his feet and taking him through the crowd, toward the building. He went struggling to gain his footing, and tugging his arms when the men tightened their grip.

Thomas returned his attention to the young homeless man. "What's your name, good fellow?" He helped the man stand, taking notice of his matted hair, overgrown beard, and wrinkled clothes. They were worn and tattered black articles caked with dirt from the city sidewalk. Thomas put his arm through the young man's. "Don't be shy, you have a story, and it deserves to be heard."

The crowd hushed when the man cleared his throat to speak. Patricia and Mary took center front, facing the man who saved their lives as they knew it. "My name's Hawk. I just did what I knew was right."

"How did you know?" a woman called from the crowd. "Like, what made you even know to act?"

Hawk lowered his eyes to stare at the sidewalk. "I was trained."

"What do you mean?" Patricia asked. "Trained how? You're so young."

Hawk shook his head. "I'm twenty-one, be twenty-two tomorrow. I was a security officer at Braxton's." He glanced up at Patricia, then at Thomas, who nodded for him to continue. "I lost my job the first year of Covid lockdowns. My company folded. It wasn't a large organization, and I couldn't afford my apartment."

Patricia pursed her lips. "There was a freeze on evictions and foreclosures. If they did, it was illegal."

"Illegal activities happen every day, all day. There is no discrimination when it comes to who and what, just a matter of when and where. I was in my third year at the University for criminal justice, but losing my job and home meant I had to drop out." Hawk shrugged. "I've been living on the streets since."

"Why didn't you go to a shelter?" Patricia asked.

Thomas made eye contact with her and raised his brow to show her the irony of the situation. "There must have been someplace you could have gone. Family, friends?"

Hawk sighed, "This was the Covid lockdown. People panicked. No one wanted to invite you into their house. They couldn't afford to maintain their own household, let

alone take in a stranger. And as for the shelters, well, let me explain something I learned the hard way. There are rules."

Mary wiped the tears on her cheek and asked in a broken voice, "Why don't you follow them?"

"I did and do. But Chicago alone has less than forty homeless shelters and over half the state's homeless population. The last time I checked, there were over a hundred thousand people. Not all of us are criminals. I've met women who fled abusive homes, kids who ran away from lives that were worse than any condition they experienced on the streets, and grown men who lost their minds after serving time in the military. They just want to live alone, not be bothered, and not have to deal with life. I would give up a room at a shelter every time, if it meant a woman, child, or veteran had a warm bed for the night. I'm young, I manage." Hawk glanced at Mary. "To directly answer your question, we are not allowed to stay consecutively or for extended periods of time. Some shelters let you stay three nights, others thirty days in an apartment like flat, but they prefer to have families that might be able to get back on their feet. Guys like me are not greeted kindly."

Patricia's jaw dropped. "Did you say only forty shelters? And over a hundred thousand people? That would mean... wait. How many rooms are there?"

Hawk shook his head again. "No rooms, just beds. There are maybe thirty-five thousand beds in the country."

"You mean county," Mary said.

"No, in the country. As you can see, it doesn't give us

a chance. It's more like a lottery win. Anyway, those guys who grabbed your daughter are traffickers. Chicago is a hub for child trafficking, and I saw the signs. The van, the way they went directly for her with a plan. The streets are rough no matter what the neighborhood. I wanted to be a state policeman, but after spending three years on the streets, I'm thinking I want to go into social work, focus on people like me, and get them integrated back into society. I also want to help put an end to the heinous acts men like the man I caught are part of. It sickens me that I can't see a way to help right now."

Thomas folded his arms as the police sirens grew louder. "Hawk, I'm going to offer you a deal. I will pay for you to finish school, through a graduate degree."

"What?" the young man gasped.

"No," Patricia said. "The least I can do is pay for your tuition and on campus housing." She took out her cell. "I am securing a room for you at the hotel near my complex. You can stay there until you receive your acceptance and matriculate. I want updates on your grades and your word that you will follow through. You saved my daughter's life. There is no price tag that can pay you back for that."

"I don't know what to say," Hawk said. His voice broke, tears caught in the reddish whiskers that decorated his cheeks and chin. His hands trembled. He stuck them in his pants pockets. Phone lights lit the sidewalk as people recorded videos and took snapshots of the moment.

The police arrived and wove their way through the

crowd toward Hawk, Thomas, Patricia, and Mary. An ambulance soon followed. The crowd dispersed after the officers pulled Patricia aside to question her and Mary. A separate duo stayed with Hawk.

"If it wasn't for that young man, I don't know what would have happened to my daughter. It's a shame that a great city like Chicago suffers from all this crime and homelessness. I shouldn't have to worry about leaving the township building with my child. These people need to be stopped," Patricia reprimanded.

"Yes, ma'am," the female officer said. "Now, Mary. Have you ever seen these men before? Do you recognize the vehicle?"

Mary shook her head to answer in the negative.

After an hour and a barrage of questions. Hawk was free to go. Thomas, Patricia, and Mary stayed with him until the crowd dispersed, which started once the officers were on scene. As Thomas suspected, Hawk's intervention was considered a citizen's arrest and did not warrant any further investigation into his actions. They took the detained man into custody, loading him into the backseat of a police car. The van was caught on surveillance footage and by a pedestrian who witnessed the incident from the township building. They had it on video.

It was moments like those that made Thomas grateful for modern technology.

The bystander lingered back when the people rolled along to their cars and dwellings. He had a gray business

suit, thick, black-framed glasses, and long dreads pulled back in a pony. His black converse sneakers stood out from the rest of him. He approached Hawk and Thomas.

"Well done, young man," he said.

Hawk nodded. "Wish it wasn't necessary, to be honest, but thank you."

The stranger spread his arms, motioning to the surrounding buildings. "Is it right, you have no family?"

"I was too ashamed of my situation to tell them. I came here to make something of myself and lost it all. The only thing my parents ever wanted was for me to go to college and not have to struggle like they did. I come from a line of farmers. They invested in me, and I failed them. It was easier to go off the record."

"Whereabouts are you from?" he asked.

"About two and half hours away in Peoria County, sir."

"How did a young man from Hamilton County learn to tackle like that? You knew what you were doing before you even had him on the ground."

"Well, I studied Brazilian Jujitsu and earned my black belt when I was fifteen."

"I tell you what, Hawk. You get yourself cleaned up and have a good night's sleep." He fished a business card from his pocket. "You come see me tomorrow. Call and I'll have a driver pick you up. And get yourself some new digs before you check into that hotel the nice lady was offering. It just so happens to be that I've got an opening on my security team. The job is yours if you want it."

Hawk smiled, his eyes glinting from the streetlights and over-pouring emotions. "Yes, sir. Thank you." But then he ran his hand over his unkempt hair and face.

"You get washed up and I'll have the driver stop at a barber on your way. No worries, young man. Nothing in life comes free and you've paid your dues. I'll see you tomorrow." The stranger walked toward a Rolls Royce and climbed in.

Hawk turned the card over in his hand. "R.W. Trading."

"That is one of Chicago's wealthiest businessmen. He has connections around the world. You get your education and stick with him, and I wouldn't be surprised if you travelled the globe."

Patricia put her hand on the homeless man's shoulder. "Hawk, you have a room ready for you tonight. You can stay there. It's the Kildare. I'm going to take Mary home. This night has been too long." She turned to Thomas. "You have my support, Mr. Thomas. I intend to take part in the betterment of our community outreach programs. And like Hawk's new employer, I promise to do more. Actions speak louder than a check."

"Thank you, Patricia. If you're interested, there's a benefit concert next month, here in the square. It's part of a new scholarship program." Thomas smiled at Mary. "I believe you may know my headliner. Ever heard of the Foo Fighters? David Grohl is a friend."

Mary smiled at her mother. "They are awesome!"

"Then I guess we have a concert to attend." Patricia

took Mary's hand and led her to their car. It was a mere five hundred feet from where the van stopped, grabbing the innocent preteen. "I hadn't realized just how close they were to us. It's frightening."

"With the footage from the street cams and the bystander's recording, I think we gave the trafficking ring a sore dent. Let's hope it leads to many arrests and even more girls found," Hawk said. "If I had to do it over, I would have liked to be on a task force aimed at taking down the people responsible."

Thomas patted the man on the back. "It's never too late to help."

CHAPTER 11

New Dawn

Thomas was filled with a sense of pride and excitement as he stood outside the building for the ribbon cutting ceremony. He had accomplished something he had always dreamed of, and he couldn't wait to see it in action. He had invited the local media to attend the opening ceremony, hoping that the publicity would help them get more donations and volunteers. It was his first full-service shelter. A full circle entity, unlike any other in the country.

He was overjoyed to see his daughter and grandchildren standing next to three new faces: Patricia, Mary, and Hawk. The young man was clean shaven, had a barbered cut, and wore a tailored suit. When he looked over his shoulder at Elize and the rest of the committee members, he realized the reality had hit them all. True happiness existed in their service. Each member held a pair of scissors.

"I can't believe the board was unanimous," Elize said.

"I think the events that unfolded showed them that homeless people are still people. It was the push they needed," the treasurer said. She had her scissors poised.

The news people had their cameras set on tripods while the reporters read over their questions. More than a hundred people turned out for the ceremony. They filled the street, which the police had closed. A detour directed the traffic around the growing crowd. Thomas was delighted

with the turnout and hoped it meant more volunteers. But in reality, he knew they were taking away knowledge and wonder. Some would want to know how to start their own nonprofit service, others would wonder why the need was so great. In the end, they would research it or have their curiosity peak and rekindled at the next event.

Thomas hoped he would be part of that. As a matter of personal interest, he was looking into expanding his own mission. Nonprofit, no cost, medical facilities, and improving the foster care system were on his agenda. But that was for a different time, a different day. Right now, he was going to celebrate the first victory of his retirement.

He laughed to himself, *Retirement!* He knew himself too well to know that he would not rest. Rest was for the weary, Thomas felt invigorated. He had an upcoming fundraising concert with David Grohl in the works and received phone calls from other celebrities wanting to do their part.

David had informed him that the lineup would include three headliners, including himself, and some amazing young talents—all from Chicago. "Yo, Thomas, my man. I got to thinking, the people of Chicago need to be reminded what a great city it is. We all have our roots there, and for the first benefit, we want it to be a hometown reunion."

Thomas was floored by the news. "This is going to be big; you know that."

"I don't do small," the rock-star said. "You remember the eighties when they had that *We are the World* concert and people around the world held hands?"

"Oh my gosh, I do," Thomas said. "Are you old enough for that?"

David laughed, a full-throated sound. One that let Thomas know he was flattered, but still wasn't going to answer. "Even if I told you, you wouldn't believe me."

"Try me," Thomas joked. "I'm no spring chicken."

"Please, my grandma's got a decade on you, easy."

The two men laughed.

Thomas coughed. "Well, it doesn't really matter, does it? These kids need to see that they have a future. Maybe not all will make it in Los Angeles, but if they are determined, the city has opportunities waiting."

"That's exactly why I invited sixteen of their own. I know how they think. When you believe there is no way out of your situation, you look for a way. The only thing that matters is not staying where you are." David said.

David and Thomas's phone call ended with a promise to meet for dinner in a month. That was about when the show was scheduled.

Mary ran up to Thomas and held his hand. "You look like you were thinking about something important."

Thomas smiled. "I was."

She reached up to whisper in his ear, "I was thinking about something important, too."

"Oh, yeah?" he said. "What was yours?"

"I want to help, just like you. Someday, I'm going to make sure everyone has a place to go. What was yours?"

"That I can't wait to cheer you on."

#

When the first guests arrived, Thomas was surprised by how emotional he felt. He spent so much time and energy garnering acceptance for this place that he forgot the joy of witnessing a dream come to fruition. The guests were grateful and kind, and Thomas knew that he and the committee had made the right decision.

Over the next few months, the shelter became a beacon of hope for the homeless community in Chicago. They served hundreds of meals a day, provided warm beds for people to sleep in, and even offered job training and counseling services. There were nurse practitioners and doctors who donated their time. All of the volunteers worked tirelessly, but they were rewarded by seeing the impact they were having on people's lives—community lives.

Of course, there were challenges along the way. There were funding issues, and they had to deal with zoning laws and building codes. There were also disagreements among the volunteers about how things should be done. But Thomas always managed to keep everyone focused on the ultimate goal: helping those in need. He planned to hand the reins over to Elize, who watched and learned better than any intern or apprentice he had ever taught in his many years of community betterment.

#

As the months turned into years, the shelter continued to grow and evolve. More services and programs were

added, which helped countless people get back on their feet. Thomas was proud of what he had accomplished, but he knew it wouldn't have been possible without the support of his team.

The team was an essential part of success. He knew the right people to appoint to the right jobs. The right questions to ask, and the right approaches. He never allowed a hiccup in politics or differences in opinion stop him in his philanthropic endeavors. Looking back, Thomas knew that buying that dilapidated brick building had been one of the best decisions of his life. It had allowed him to create something truly meaningful and make a positive impact on the world. He had learned so much along the way, not just about construction and management, but about compassion, empathy, and the power of community. He always knew the power, but standing right there standing among the smiling faces, sipping hot coffee, and signing up for services, there was change. And it was all due to the collaboration of an incredible committee with grit and determination who helped bring it all to life.

From the time Thomas was a young teenager, he knew his purpose in life was to help others—to use his own skills, knowledge, and assets to make every place he went better than before. Walking through the shelter, greeting the guests and volunteers, and feeling the fulfillment of it all gave him gratitude. He was thankful for his position in life to help those suffering.

But even as he looked into the future, Thomas knew

that there was still so much work to be done. Homelessness was a complex issue, and he knew he couldn't solve it on his own. He hoped that his shelter could be a model for others, inspiring people to take action and make a difference in their own communities.

The old brick building that had once been a symbol of decay and neglect was now a place of hope and possibility. And it was all thanks to the vision and dedication of one man who refused to give up on his dream.

Thomas walked out of the shelter, taking a deep breath of fresh air. The sun was setting, and the sky was painted in shades of orange and pink. He looked back at the building, feeling a sense of pride wash over him. It was something that would continue to make a difference in people's lives long after he was gone. It was a legacy that he could be proud of. But he also knew that he couldn't rest on his laurels. There were still people out there who needed his help. People who were struggling to survive on the streets, with no place to call home.

Thomas made a promise to himself that he would continue to fight for the homeless, to advocate for their rights and work towards finding long-term solutions to the issue of homelessness. He knew it wouldn't be easy, but he also knew that he had the support of his team and the wider community. As he walked towards his car, Thomas couldn't help but feel an even greater gratitude for everything that had led him to this point. The hardships, the setbacks, and the moments of doubt had all been worth it.

He had inspired the creation of something beautiful out of nothing, and it was a testament to the power of the human spirit.

He got into his car and drove away, feeling content and fulfilled. He knew that the road ahead would be long and winding, but he was ready to continue facing it head-on. He had a purpose, a mission, and he was determined to see it come to light. There were others out there, just like him, who believed that everyone deserved a safe and secure place to call home, a warm meal, and someone willing to listen.

Epilogue

The question has been asked of me many times. Why or how did you get into nonprofit work? I remember when I was sixteen years old and had a friend in my class at school who was diagnosed with cancer. It seemed like one day he was in class and the next he wasn't. It was my first experience with someone young who had died. It broke my heart. I knew his family well and they were grieving and trying to grasp what had happened. One night I made the decision that I was going to do something for this family.

As I weighed different options for putting on an event, little did I know that this event would be the first of what is now over 250 events that I have been a part of. With the help of a friend, we ended up raising around $3500 for his family. It wasn't the amount of money we raised that was the cool part; it was the feeling I vividly remember as we handed them a check. It was like handing them hope at a time when they needed it most. To me it felt like a million dollars.

I wanted to have that feeling of helping others again, and my mind was always racing with ideas to help others. Even with college around the corner, the fundraising

and events didn't stop. As I look back to what seems like yesterday, I always hope positive change were made.

This is not a 'me' thing—it is about lives impacted for those in need. It is about having empathy and the hope that our world and communities can become stronger. People who choose this line of work need to be commended. They work tirelessly to help others and we need more of them. We need more educators, therapists, counselors, nurses, and nonprofit people. We need our youth to become the leaders our communities need. We must become better as a whole.

I'll debate with anybody who feels it is not their job to take care of the community they live in. We all have a responsibility to make our world better. Is it not your job to have passion for where you live and compassion for the people you work, interact, and live with? We all are guilty of judging people or actions of others. Have you ever considered that the person next to you at work is not smiling because they have a family member with cancer, or their mom just passed, or they have no food at home? My point is that you do not know what is going on in most people's lives.

We need to be humble, loving, and have the faith in others that, they too, are trying to get better and want to get better. Our society has become so divided—why? My challenge to you is to have more empathy, care about your surroundings and want to understand situations before judgment occurs. Some people say to me that we are all

too far gone. Do not believe that ignorant statement. That statement is for quitters.

My challenge to you is to:
1. Stop the hate.
2. Stop the bullying.
3. Do something good every day for someone and then yourself.
4. Have manners.
5. Understand you are a role model to someone.
6. Find that empathy within you.
7. Have passion for something and compassion for all.
8. Not be afraid to ask for help.
9. Be a change agent.
10. Have Faith.

If we all work on even some of these points, wouldn't we all be on our way to *Changing Lives and Saving Lives Daily?*

You have my word—I am also working every day on becoming a better person, too. Let's do it together.

Matt George
The Nonprofit Prophet

Matt George

Matt George hails from Peoria, Illinois. He is an author, a Harvard Business School Executive Leadership Coach, President of employeeInsite, entrepreneur, consultant, television host, public speaker, and influencer.

As the former President/CEO of several leading nonprofits, Matt saw social service agencies most serious social ills. Matt draws from over thirty years of front-line experience to fearlessly act as an agent for change and defender of good against the gnawing grind of social decay, poverty, homelessness, and crime. From running a $35-million-dollar company with over 450 employees, to handling some of the toughest cases in business and social service, Matt is a trustworthy and confident leader who commands a room and loves to see others win. Matt is now taking the message globally that it is all of our jobs to take care of the communities that we live in.

Matt is also a popular TV host, hosting his own weekly half-hour television show, "Business Forward", and author of the #1 Amazon bestselling book *Nonprofit Game Plan: The Proven Strategy for Nonprofit Success*. Matt changes the

narrative of poorly run 501c3 charities looking for handouts and uses his unorthodox style and proven results to solidify the case that nonprofits should run like businesses, not charities. And now Matt has taken that approach in helping all businesses achieve their goals. Former Caterpillar Inc. CEO and Chairman of the Board, Doug Oberhelman says, "Matt exemplifies leadership in his community and making it a much better place. He's involved, committed, and is recognized for his many contributions. His ability to lead large complex organizations are well documented and many people look up to him."

Kevin Harrington, an original Shark from the hit TV show Shark Tank and inventor of the infomercial, calls Matt "the Nonprofit CEO of our time." He states that "Matt George is undoubtedly a community leader & organizer with unbreakable resilience, compassion, and a huge heart. His empathetic approach offers a 24/7 open door policy with an ear to listen and a shoulder to cry on."

Living by the motto "Impossible is for the Unwilling" and driven to be "All In, All the Time," Matt stays true to his calling by embodying his own mission statement that "Every day there is an opportunity to *Change Lives and Save Lives*."

Matt and his wife Laura live in Peoria, Illinois and have five children, Carly, Allie, Lauren, Izabelle, and Matthew.

CONTACT INFORMATION

Email: info@themattgeorge.com

Linkedin: the-matt-george

Instagram: @therealmattgeorge

Facebook page: @themattgeorge

Twitter: @themattgeorge

Tiktok: @therealmattgeorge

Website: themattgeorge.com

www.ingramcontent.com/pod-product-compliance
Lightning Source LLC
Chambersburg PA
CBHW070808280326
41934CB00012B/3109

* 9 7 9 8 8 8 5 8 1 1 0 8 8 *